THE
GOOD
LAND

JOHN ECKHARDT

CHARISMA HOUSE

Visit the author's website at www.johneckhardt.global.

Library of Congress Cataloging-in-Publication Data
Names: Eckhardt, John, 1957- author.
Title: The good land / by John Eckhardt.
Description: Lake Mary, Florida : Charisma House, [2020] | Includes
  bibliographical references.
Identifiers: LCCN 2019029545 (print) | LCCN 2019029546 (ebook) | ISBN
  9781629996882 (trade paperback) | ISBN 9781629996899 (ebook)
Subjects: LCSH: Kingdom of God--Biblical teaching. | Spiritual
  life--Biblical teaching. | Christian life. | Palestine--In the Bible. |
  Land tenure--Biblical teaching.
Classification: LCC BT94 .E245 2020 (print) | LCC BT94 (ebook) | DDC
  231.7/2--dc23
LC record available at https://lccn.loc.gov/2019029545
LC ebook record available at https://lccn.loc.gov/2019029546

This publication is translated in Spanish under the title *La buena tierra*, copyright © 2020 by John Eckhardt, published by Casa Creación, a Charisma Media company. All rights reserved.

19 20 21 22 23 — 987654321
Printed in the United States of America

CONTENTS

Introduction

THE GOOD LAND REVELATION

THE MESSAGE I share in this book began as a prophetic word during a Tuesday night service at the church I pastor, Crusaders Church in Chicago. I prophesied about moving into a good land. After delivering that word, I began to do a word study in the Scriptures regarding "the land"—the land of Canaan, the Promised Land, inheriting the land, and the good land. I did more study on this subject than I had before, and what I discovered developed into a small e-book I released in 2018 and has now been expanded into this book you hold in your hand. I believe that the revelation in this book will stir your faith and encourage you to live in the promises of God.

I like Bible word studies that lead me to look at the Scriptures in a new way. In many of my books I have taken on certain words or concepts derived from popular verses that we have gotten familiar with and presented them with fresh revelation about what God is saying to His people today. Hebrews 4:12 says that God's Word is "living and active" (TLV), which essentially means that any part of it can take on a new meaning for you and your life as you involve the Spirit of God in your study or devotional time. It also means that you can receive such powerful revelation that you are convicted to believe differently, which many times can lead to a new life in God even if you have been following Him for many years.

This has happened for me over and over again. The Spirit of God comes alive through the Scriptures and allows us to grow from faith to faith and glory to glory as we read and study the Scriptures.

Have you ever found yourself reading a scripture you know or have heard many times in church, but on that particular day its meaning becomes brand-new to you? How far have you taken that revelation? When this happens to me, I am inclined to go deeper into God's Word to see what else He wants to show me concerning the word or idea. I then look for all the ways the word has been used in Scripture, and many times the revelation is so significant that I feel led to preach sermons, write books, and host conferences and webinars just off that one word. Both my Asaph Worship Gatherings and Chayil Conference were developed out of a fresh revelation of familiar scriptures.

Biblical word studies help broaden our understanding of the living and active Word of God. We should always be looking for and expecting new revelation when we come to read and study God's Word. When you look at how certain words are used throughout Scripture, examining the Greek, Hebrew, and Aramaic meanings, you will get a greater understanding of biblical truths.

The revelation of the good land God provides both spiritually and physically for His people is one such revelation that I believe will challenge your faith and cause you to expect and experience greater breakthrough in many areas of your life. Other concepts that stood out to me when I studied the words *good* and *land* in Scripture were "fat and fatness" and "the finest of wheat." Good land is such that produces the finest and most abundant harvests—spiritual, financial, and more; a secure, peaceful, and prosperous home, one that testifies of the faithfulness and glory of God in a believer's life. As we enter this study on the good land, be ready to receive a new perspective on prosperity and the blessings of the Lord.

What Is the Good Land?

The good land is a picture of the kingdom, kingdom living, living in Zion, living in the glory realm, and living in the promises of God. The good land is God's country. It is a place where goodness, abundance, prosperity, excellence, refreshing, beauty, nourishment, blessing, satisfaction, plenty, and glory are ways of life. It is the land of the finest, best, and choicest of meat and grain. It is a place where we are nourished, shielded, and safe. We receive abundant harvests, and all our works are fruitful in the good land. It is a place where becoming fat and large is a spiritual picture of prosperity, wealth, and the anointing. I have a passion to see people live in prosperity, abundance, peace, joy, and victory in the land that God has promised us in Christ.

The first time the words *land* and *good* are mentioned in Scripture is in connection with gold: "And the gold of that land is good: there is bdellium and the onyx stone" (Gen. 2:12). Gold represents wealth and prosperity. Many believers fail to recognize that heaven is a wealthy place! There is no poverty there. There is no famine there. There is no despair there. Prosperity includes finances but is not restricted to finances.

Blessing, redemption, and restoration also dwell here. We inherit and enjoy the promises of God in the good land. As I studied the Scripture passages where the words *good* and *land* are used together, I received a revelation of the peace, joy, and righteousness we can experience when we understand that, because of Christ, we dwell in the good land.

The good land is also a picture of the Promised Land, to which God was leading the Israelites upon their exodus from Egypt. He was leading them to the physical place called

Canaan. God Himself brought them into a good land, a land of milk and honey (Exod. 3:8; Num. 14:8; Deut. 31:20; Ezek. 20:15), as He promised their forefather Abraham (Gen. 12:7).

Today God's people enter the good land through Jesus Christ, as we have now by faith become the spiritual seed of Abraham (Rom. 11:11–31). The good land is no longer a physical place but is now a spiritual representation of what was purchased for us by the finished work of Jesus at the cross. It is a metaphor for our spiritual inheritance in Christ and the blessings we have as a result. So now because of Christ the saints of God dwell in this land and possess it by faith.

As we enter the good land by faith, it is important to recognize that faith begins by understanding and accepting the promises of God. Faith declares the promises, stands on the promises, and fights hell with the promises. This is a key to entering the good land, because it is the land of promise where we inherit and enjoy all the promises of God, where the promises of God are yes and amen (2 Cor. 1:20). Jesus made a way for us to enter into the promises of God. He is the doorway and provides unlimited access. Imagine a spiritual all-access pass! This is a prophetic picture of what Jesus did for us so we could enter into all of His promises.

Again, through Christ we become citizens of the good land. We are called to walk by faith and not by sight (natural vision). When we understand the realm of faith, we can partner with heaven to enter into that land.

> Now to Abraham and his seed were the promises made. He saith not, and to seeds, as of many; but as of one, and to thy seed, which is Christ.
>
> —GALATIANS 3:16

And if ye be Christ's, then are ye Abraham's seed, and heirs according to the promise.

—GALATIANS 3:29

Our Inheritance

Blessed are the meek: for they shall inherit the earth.

—MATTHEW 5:5

Earth in the Bible's original Greek language is *ge*, which literally means "land."[1] That's a big distinction, because when you hear or read the word *earth*, you may think about the whole planet—the global earth, that the meek will inherit the entire planet, but when you think of land, the concept of the physical area adjusts to mean only a portion or a part of the planet. Of course, when God sent the Israelites in to possess the land, they were not going in to possess the entire planet. They were possessing the land of Canaan—their "earth"—from the Brook of Egypt to the Mediterranean Sea to Mount Hor, the Sea of Galilee to the Jordan River and the Dead Sea. God gave them parameters. (See Numbers 34:1–12.)

When Jesus said in Matthew 5:5 that the meek will inherit the earth, He had certain spiritual boundary lines in mind. Though the verse is commonly quoted, there is a lot more to it than meets the eye. He did not mean the entire physical planet but a special spiritual land set aside for those who love Him that they inherit as they come into fellowship with Him.

Let me share with you several scriptures that talk about the good land. One is Psalm 25:13. It says, "His soul shall dwell at ease; and his seed shall *inherit the earth* [the land]" (emphasis added). The rest are all found in Psalm 37, where the phrase *inherit the earth* (or *land*) is mentioned five times. This is a powerful psalm, as it begins with, "Fret not thyself because of evildoers, neither be thou envious against the workers of iniquity. For they shall soon be cut down like the grass, and wither as the green herb. Trust in the LORD, and do good; so shalt thou dwell in the land, and verily thou shalt be fed" (vv. 1–3). Jesus is quoting from Psalm 37 when He says in Matthew 5:5, "Blessed are the meek: for they shall inherit the earth."

Let's take a look at those five verses now:

> For evildoers shall be cut off: but those that wait upon the LORD, they shall *inherit the earth* [the land].
> —Psalm 37:9, emphasis added

This is the verse Jesus quoted in Matthew 5:

> But the meek shall *inherit the earth* [the land]; and shall delight themselves in the abundance of peace [*shalom*].
> —Psalm 37:11, emphasis added

> For such as be blessed of him shall *inherit the earth* [the land]; and they that be cursed of him shall be cut off.
> —Psalm 37:22, emphasis added

The following two verses actually use the words *the land*:

> The righteous shall *inherit the land*, and dwell therein for ever.
> —Psalm 37:29, emphasis added

> Wait on the LORD, and keep his way, and he shall exalt thee to *inherit the land*: when the wicked are cut off, thou shalt see it.
> —Psalm 37:34, emphasis added

So what is this about inheriting the land? First, I believe that all the promises of God are fulfilled in Christ. Christ is the fulfillment of all the old covenant promises and all the old covenant types and symbols. As part of the old covenant, God told the Israelites, "I am going to bring you into a good land. This is going to be your inheritance. This will be your possession." (See Deuteronomy 5:31, 6:1, and 26:1.) But the inheritance of the physical land was something that was temporary, earthly, physical, and natural. It was a type of something greater, which we find in Christ.

Understanding Biblical Types and Shadows

It is important in terms of rightly dividing the Word of God to know the difference between the types and symbols and the fulfillment that is in Christ. All the old types and symbols: Israel, the land, the mountain, the feasts—Passover, Pentecost, Tabernacles, the priesthood, the sacrifices…All these things were types and shadows of a greater reality in which the fulfillment is Christ.

So when Scripture says, "The meek shall inherit the earth," or, "The righteous shall inherit the land," it is an old covenant picture of what we inherit in Christ. The land is Christ; Christ is the Promised Land. Christ is our inheritance. So blessings, prosperity, peace, shalom, favor, land flowing with milk and honey—all these are types and symbols of what it means to live in Christ and to walk and live in the Spirit.

What is interesting is that the Book of Psalms was written almost one thousand years after Joshua led the people of Israel into Canaan, but still we find several references in Psalm 37 to inheriting the land. Why would the Spirit of God through the psalmist talk about inheriting the earth when it is hundreds of years removed from when Joshua came into the land? Why is the Word of God still talking about possessing the earth?

Then in Matthew 5, fifteen hundred or so years removed from Moses and Joshua, Jesus again talks about inheriting the earth. Evidently Israel did not possess the land, the earth—or God was referring to something much greater than the physical land or the physical earth.

Could it be that the good land is about the Spirit of God

drawing our focus to something greater than a physical land? This is very important because so many people today, especially Christians, are focused on the Middle East, a physical piece of land—what happens in Israel, the Gaza Strip, and Palestine—as if that is to be the focus of the kingdom. They miss the fact that the land that God sent Israel into—and please catch this because you must understand types, shadows, and figures in order to rightly divide the Word of God—is a natural representation of something much greater in the spirit. Though they were sent into this physical land, we must understand that God has something much bigger in mind than just a physical piece of land. The kingdom of heaven is much bigger than that.

Receiving this broadened perspective can be a problem for some Christians whose eyes are so locked on the natural and the physical that they miss the spiritual reality of what we possess in Christ.

Could it be that the land the Israelites were told to possess was a picture of something much greater, something we now possess in Christ? I believe that it is. What we possess in Christ is a fulfillment of the picture and shadow of what the people of Israel possessed by going into a physical land. So literally Christ is the good land—living in Christ. Living in the Spirit is the good land, and that is the land given to us.

Allow me to lead you through an example of how a type and shadow may be read in the Old Testament and then seen in the New Testament as fulfilled. The Book of Deuteronomy says this:

> For the LORD your God is bringing you into a good land, a land of brooks of *water*, of fountains and springs, that flow out of valleys and hills.
> —DEUTERONOMY 8:7, NKJV, EMPHASIS ADDED

What does water represent in the Bible? It represents the Spirit of God. Jesus said in John 7:38, referring to the believer, "Out of his belly shall flow rivers of living water." And in John 4 He said, "The water that I shall give him shall be in him a well of water springing up into everlasting life" (v. 14).

The good land is a picture of living a Spirit-filled life—worship, prophecy, words of knowledge and wisdom, discernment, tongues, interpretation, miracles, the gifts of the Spirit, life in the Spirit. This is the good land. Flowing in the Spirit, operating in the Spirit—that's the good land. That's what we have in Christ. Life should never be boring when you have the Spirit of God flowing consistently. Your life should be full of water, full of fountains, full of depth, and full of the river of God (Ps. 46:4). The water of the Spirit of God should always be flowing in your life; if you are not experiencing that, you are not living in the good land. And if you allow it, the enemy will rob you of what it means to live in the good land, to live in the blessings of the Spirit of God.

As you study the land and see all the things the people of Israel inherited, realize that these are types and shadows of what you have in Christ. So when Christ says, "Blessed are the meek: for they shall inherit the earth" (Matt. 5:5), He is not referring to something physical; He is referring to something much greater than the physical. He is referring to kingdom living, living in Christ, salvation, redemption, deliverance, healing, abundance, worship, glory, joy, peace, and shalom. This is the good land.

The Meek

Blessed are the meek: for they shall inherit the earth.

—MATTHEW 5:5

If you are wondering who "the meek" are, let me uncover the mystery: you are the meek. The good land is part of your inheritance in Christ. You are blessed and an heir to the land. It is yours in Christ!

The meek inherit the earth (land). They delight themselves in abundant prosperity. The meek can have the best.

> But the meek shall inherit the land, and delight themselves in abundant prosperity.
> —Psalm 37:11, nrsv

The land that God gives is the best. This is called God's country. The obedient, favored, meek, and wise enjoy the best and finest in God's country. They are those who fear the Lord, hear His voice, and do what He says. God will feed them from the best of the land.

> Then you will have joy in the Lord. I will cause you to ride on the high places of the earth. And I will feed you with the best from the land given to your father Jacob. The mouth of the Lord has spoken.
> —Isaiah 58:14, nlv

"The best" is a part of the inheritance of the saints that comes through the seed of Abraham, which is Christ Himself. The King James Version says, "[I will] feed thee with the heritage of Jacob." This is a good inheritance or a rich legacy (Ps. 16:6). Our heritage as the spiritual seed of Abraham, now grafted in, is the best.

We can now eat of the finest of wheat and of the fat, which is the Lord's portion of the best sacrifice. The fat was important to God. The people of Israel were commanded to offer the fat as a sacrifice. (See Leviticus 3:14 and Numbers 18:17.) In the coming chapters we will explore the significance of the fat and fatness as it pertains to entering into the good land and into God's best.

The meek are humble, teachable, and able to be corrected by God. They are willing and obedient; therefore, they eat the good of the land (Isa. 1:19).

When you read the phrase "blessed are the meek," know that it is all about Jesus and our being restored through salvation to His image and likeness. Jesus is a picture of the meek. In Matthew 11:29 He said He was meek and lowly in heart. He has inherited the earth in the sense that He possesses the entire world.

Psalm 2:8 says, "Ask of Me, and I will give You the nations for Your inheritance, and the ends of the earth for Your possession" (NKJV). This verse tells of the promise of the Father to the Son, who becomes the King. Christ's dominion is over the entire earth. Jesus is the embodiment of meekness, and when we enter into Christ, we take on all that He is; therefore, we take on His meekness. His meekness becomes part of our lives. We cannot be meek apart from Christ.

All the promises that are revealed to us through Scripture and by the Spirit of God are found and fulfilled in Christ. So blessed are the meek—blessed are those who are in Christ, the meek One—for they shall inherit the earth, or possess the land.

A Place of Freedom

In all that God did to bring Israel out of bondage and into a good land, a picture is painted of how God views His children, how much He loves to bring freedom to them. In fact everything about God screams freedom! The Bible says, "Where the Spirit of the Lord is, there is freedom" (2 Cor. 3:17, NIV). The anointing, which is likened to the olive oil that flows freely in the good land, destroys the yokes! It undoes and shatters all that has tied you to bondage. This is one reason the enemy hates the power of the anointing. It will bring you out of heaviness and oppression. God's presence and glory are in the good land. There is freedom in His glory, which cannot be separate from His presence. They are one and the same. You cannot be in God's presence and stay bound.

> And I am come down to deliver them out of the hand of the Egyptians, and to bring them up out of that land unto a good land and a large, unto a land flowing with milk and honey; unto the place of the Canaanites, and the Hittites, and the Amorites, and the Perizzites, and the Hivites, and the Jebusites.
>
> —Exodus 3:8

God does not want to just bring you out of bondage; He wants to bring you into a good and prosperous place where freedom reigns. It is a twofold action. You are first brought out of the land of bondage and oppression and then led into the land of promise. You are delivered to move into the good land. You are delivered to go into a large place, a wealthy place.

> Thou hast caused men to ride over our heads; we went through fire and through water: but thou broughtest us out into a wealthy place.
>
> —Psalm 66:12

The good land is a land without scarceness. There is no lack. God's abundance flows freely in the good land.

> A land wherein thou shalt eat bread without scarceness, thou shalt not lack any thing in it; a land whose stones are iron, and out of whose hills thou mayest dig brass.
>
> —Deuteronomy 8:9

Appropriated by Faith

Without a revelation of Christ, of who Jesus is, you will not get the revelation of the good land, nor will you be able to dwell in it. Unfortunately many believers accept Christ without knowing who He really is. Christ is our good land.

Do you remember when Jesus asked the disciples, "Who do men say that I, the Son of Man, am?" (Matt. 16:13, NKJV)? When Peter finally answered Jesus' next question, "Who do you say that I am?" (v. 15), we are witness to Peter's revelation of who Jesus is: "You are the Christ, the Son of the living God" (v. 16, NKJV). My desire is that people get a revelation of Christ and thereby get a revelation of the good land.

Many believers have not allowed themselves to live in the good land because of tradition, religion, fear, doubt, unbelief, and other people who don't want to live in the good land and will block them from entering into it even though the Bible says they will inherit the earth—the land. They never use their faith to appropriate this.

So I've written this book—*The Good Land*—to teach you how to inherit the full promises of God by faith and a revelation of Christ. I hope to stir your faith so you know what belongs to you as a child of God and how you can appropriate that by faith. Being in Christ is more than being saved. It's more than going to heaven. It's more than just being justified. There are great, great blessings, benefits, and promises that come to you as a child of God.

I want you to read this book, meditate on it, and begin to confess the promises that it contains. Believe what God is saying to you in this hour. If you are living in the bad lands, if you are not living in the good land, if you are not enjoying the fullness you have in Christ, I want you to read this book. I believe that by faith you can inherit the promises, rest, joy, peace, favor, glory, and all the great things that belong to us as a result of inheriting the land. The land does belong to you as a child of God. It is a spiritual inheritance. It is a spiritual land that belongs to you. And you can have it by faith if you understand what the land is, what it represents, and how we possess it in Christ.

I believe God wants you to live in the good land to enjoy His blessings and promises that are in Christ. The more revelation and understanding you receive, the more you confess this and believe and walk in this. Whatever your current situation is, faith will turn your whole life around. Faith will cause you to move out of a place of poverty, lack, stress, strife, heaviness, fear, and stress and into a place of victory, abundance, joy, shalom, favor, and all the promises of God that are, in Christ, yes and amen, meaning "it is so."

Don't let any church, denomination, doctrine, believer, unbeliever, or family member keep you out of the land of promise while you are living on the earth, keep you out of the blessings of God, or keep you out of the fullness of what Christ has for you. Begin to confess this and believe it, appropriating it by faith. Rise up. Come out of bondage. Come out of the wilderness. Come out of that dry place. Get into the good land and dwell there all the days of your life.

The Good Land Is for You!

The enemy will work overtime on your mind and emotions to keep you in an exhausted and frustrated state so that you will believe the good land is for super saints and not for you. This is a lie. Like many people with mega potential, there may be times when you feel stuck outside of your promises because you have unconsciously partnered with the lies of hell. This is one of Satan's strategies to get you to believe his lies, to make vows and partner with him, and to empower demon spirits to wreak havoc in your life.

You may hear words such as, "Things will never work out for you." You begin to agree with the deception and speak it over yourself: "Things will never work out for me." This is the work of the enemy, and as he influences what you speak, his demons will honor your word. They understand the realm of covenant and keep you on the outskirts of the good land by sowing lies into your heart and mind.

You must rise up, break those lies, renew your mind, and begin to prophesy the blessings of the good land. The good land is not just for others; it is for you! As a child of God you are loved, protected, and provided for. You have been stuck and depleted long enough. The enemy has zapped and drained you for far too long, but heaven has resources for every area of your life.

Refuse to accept anything less than the promises of God. Rise and believe in the goodness of God. Rise and decree that you will live in the good land. Rise and stand upon the Word of the Lord. Rise and fight the devil. Rise and worship God. Rise and move into the place of sweetness and glory, the place of peace and promise, and the place of reward. The good land is calling.

PART I

ENTERING THE GOOD LAND

Chapter 1

POSSESSING THE LAND

POSSESSING THE LAND means you control it, and if you control it, you have dominion. The land represents dominion, power, wealth, prosperity, abundance, and peace. When you possess the land and drive out the enemy, you have peace. The land then comes to represent rest.

The scriptures about the land we've been discussing so far and will discuss further are not in the Bible for you to just read. They should cause faith to arise so that you can believe enough to be motivated to lay hold of what is yours. God wants you to have your land. He wants you to have your inheritance. With the children of Israel, God gave every tribe its own land, its own place of dominion. (See Joshua 13–21.) There was enough for everyone. Just as the Israelites did, you may have to deal with giants and other enemies, but God will give you weapons to defeat them—the weapon of faith, the Word of God, the power of God, and more. He teaches our hands to war and our fingers to fight (Ps. 144:1). He will give you strategy so that you can drive out the enemy and possess what belongs to you. We will talk about this more in chapter 4, "Clearing the Land."

What we have come to discover is that prophetically Christ is the land. Through the Old Testament types and shadows we see how the people of Israel moved from a land of not

enough—Egypt—to a land of just enough—the wilderness—
to a land of more than enough—Canaan, the Promised Land,
or the good land. We get a revelation of how God will do this
for us too. He will bring us out of the world—Egypt, the land
of not enough—through the wilderness, where our needs are
just being met, but now God wants to bring us into a land of
more than enough.

This applies to you even if finances are not a problem for you.
Not everyone in the kingdom is poor or struggling financially,
but we can all use more joy, peace, good relationships, good
marriages and families, and better health and emotional well-
ness. We can all use more of the blessings, glory, power, and
favor of God in our lives that gives us an advantage over the
enemy. God wants to be your El Shaddai, the God of more
than enough. He will anoint your head with oil until your cup
overflows and runs over. The land of promise is a land of overflow, open heaven, downpour, and abundance, a land where
goodness and mercy will follow you all the days of your life.

God brought the Israelites out of Egypt through the wilderness and told them to go into the land of promise, but they
ended up staying in the wilderness for forty years. Just so you
know, it is not the will of God for you to live in the wilderness
for an extended period of time. You may be there temporarily
as God brings you out of Egypt, out of sin, and to the mountain of God, where He teaches you His Word and delivers you.

It was never the will of God for the Israelites to be in the
land for forty years. Because of their rebellion and stubborn-
ness the whole generation that was freed from Egypt ended up
dying in the wilderness. They did not have faith to endure the
short time in the wilderness as God prepared them to cross
over into Canaan. By God's grace this will not be your story.
It is God's plan for you to come out of the wilderness and cross
over into the land of promise and blessing.

Ten Keys to Possessing the Good Land

Let's go back now to Psalm 37 and some of the verses I mentioned in the introduction. I want to pull out ten keys that will help you possess the land.

1. Don't fret.

Psalm 37:1–2 says, "Do not fret because of evildoers, nor be envious of the workers of iniquity. For they shall soon be cut down like the grass, and wither as the green herb" (nkjv).

The word *fret* here means to become grieved, angry, or vexed. Through the prophet David we are being challenged by God to not be angry because of what we see or upset about what people are doing around us. God has a plan for them, and God has a plan for you. As you keep your eyes on what God has for you, trust that He is taking care of everything else. The evildoers are His business.

2. Trust in the Lord.

> Trust in the Lord, and do good; dwell in the land, and feed on His faithfulness.
>
> —Psalm 37:3, nkjv

Don't put your trust in man. I've learned this over years of ministry. Don't even put your trust in yourself. Flesh will always let you down. Put your trust in God. Focus on Him, and feed on His faithfulness. Believe Him. He is your might, strength, and power.

3. Do good.

> Trust in the Lord, and *do good*.
>
> —Psalm 37:3, emphasis added

4. Delight yourself in the Lord.

> Delight yourself also in the Lord, and He shall give you
> the desires of your heart.
>
> —PSALM 37:4, NKJV

Do you desire peace of mind; a sense of security, safety, and stability; financial provision; success in business or ministry; good relationships with family and friends; a deeper knowledge and love of God? Delight yourself—"be happy about," "make merry over," become "soft or pliable"[1]—in the things of God, and He will meet each one of your desires.

5. Commit your way to the Lord.

> Commit your way to the Lord, trust also in Him, and
> He shall bring it to pass.
>
> —PSALM 37:5, NKJV

Commit your path, plans, and purposes to the Lord, and see them lead you to the good land.

6. Rest in the Lord (Ps. 37:7).

7. Wait patiently for the Lord (Ps. 37:7, 9).

Those who wait patiently on the Lord inherit the good land.

8. Cease from anger.

> Cease from anger, and forsake wrath; do not fret—
> it only causes harm. For evildoers shall be cut off.
>
> —PSALM 37:8–9, NKJV

In Ephesians 4:26–27 the apostle Paul said, "Be ye angry, and sin not: let not the sun go down upon your wrath: neither give place to the devil." Sometimes being angry about what others are doing can be a distraction from the enemy. Again, I say, "Let God be God, and let His enemies be scattered." (See

Psalm 68:1.) Anger can oftentimes do more harm than good. You have a pursuit and purpose. Do not let the actions of others cause you to get out of step with where God is leading you. Trust Him to give you strategy to fight the battles worth fighting.

9. Be humble.

Five times in Psalm 37 the prophet David talked about inheriting the land—verses 9, 11, 22, 29, and 34—and in all five instances we see that the ones who do the inheriting are the patient, meek, and righteous. This is important.

The word *meek* in verse 11 means "humble" and "lowly."[2] We talked about this being one of the traits in the character of Christ. The meek are in essence patient because they are not anxious to have things quickly line up the way they want them to. They are not prideful and arrogant.

The righteous are by definition humble and patient, as they are in right standing with God. God is not resisting them because of their pride. They experience the grace and mercy of God, for God resists the proud but gives grace to the humble (Jas. 4:6). They wait patiently for Him because they trust His timing.

10. Embrace the glory.

> Also your people shall all be righteous; they shall inherit the land forever, the branch of My planting, the work of My hands, that I may be glorified.
>
> —Isaiah 60:21, nkjv

One of the blessings of the glory of God rising upon you, as described in Isaiah 60:1, is that God will bring you out of a place of desolation, captivity, and bondage and into the good land. When the glory of God comes, it elevates you, promotes you, and blesses you. Another benefit of the glory of God is that it brings you into a good land.

The promise of God as a result of the glory is that you will inherit the land. One of the keys to inheriting the land is letting the glory, light, excellence, brilliance, and presence of God rest on your life. The glory comes through Messiah—Christ in you, the hope of glory (Col. 1:27). Here, Isaiah is speaking to us about entering into the promise of God.

The prophets of God—David and Isaiah—shared these things from the heart of God to build our faith. The Bible says that if we believe His prophets, we will prosper (2 Chron. 20:20). Prophets have an anointing to break us into good and new things, places the enemy tries to keep us from. The devil does not want you to come into the land God has promised you. He will use any number of things to keep you bound to old places and things, or traditions and limiting beliefs. But you must break free. If you have to leave some people behind, do it. If they want to stay in the wilderness, let them stay—but you move into the good land. Use these ten keys to help you embrace the promises of God. They belong to you as a child of God.

Dispossess the Dry Land

The rebellious dwell in a dry land.

—PSALM 68:6

The meek…shall inherit the earth.

—MATTHEW 5:5

In addition to living out the ten keys above, there are things you must expel from your life if you want to live in the good land. Disobedience, pride, and rebellion will prevent you from enjoying the good life and the good land God has for you.

Anyone who is living in pride, rebellion, disobedience,

refusal to submit, or hatred of correction, authority, and accountability—and there are many who live with these things in their hearts—I guarantee you will not live in the good land. It's impossible. The Bible says the meek shall inherit the earth.

Meekness and humility are absolutely necessary if you are going to inherit the blessings and the promises of God. Many people who have allowed pride, haughtiness, and refusal to submit to godly authority into their lives are on social media. All they do is talk about the church. They don't attend church. They are not submitted to anyone. They are not submitted to a pastor. They are not accountable to anyone. They do what they want to do when they want to do it. Yet they wonder why they have not inherited the promises of God. I'm here to let you know, whether you like it or not, you will not inherit the promises of God this way.

I understand that many have been hurt by the church, but what I am talking about is submitting to godly leadership, understanding the blessing of being corrected when you are wrong. Sometimes when you are under godly leadership, God will call the leader to challenge or correct you about behavior or lifestyle choices that compromise our ability to dwell in the good land, but because of pride, rebellion, bitterness, and disobedience, that correction in love is hard to receive. Many run from this kind of accountability. They get angry. They get on Facebook, do Live broadcasts, and vent, saying the leader is religious and judgmental. Then they expect to live in the good land. It's not going to happen. The verse above says, "The meek will inherit the land, and the rebellious shall dwell in a dry land."

A dry land is the wilderness. It is the desert. It's the land where nothing grows. It is a land where there is unbearable heat during the day and blistering cold at night. It is the land of scorpions, serpents, and jackals.

I have heard people say they don't need to be accountable

to anyone but God. But God uses people and sets up human authority, which can be governmental, church, and so on. Human authority has always been established by God; you have to choose whether or not to submit to it. There are a lot of bitter, prideful, angry, rebellious people who call themselves saints and want to enjoy God's best, but they cannot because they are not meek. The meek are teachable and can be corrected. They submit and listen to proper biblical authority. They can be sat down if the authority says, "Sit down for a season."

I've never seen so many stubborn, independent, rebellious people as I have in this generation. These are people who want to live any kind of way and still come into the church to prophesy, speak in tongues, sing the song of the Lord, and do every other kind of spiritual thing in the church except submit to proper biblical authority and correction. It is the meek who will inherit the earth.

It is not often that we hear teaching about meekness and humility in the church, but it is literally the key to so much of the good things in the kingdom of God. God resists the proud but gives grace to the humble. I encourage you to get my book *Deliverance and Spiritual Warfare Manual* and study the spirit of leviathan out of Job 41. Then search your own life and see if there is any rebellion, disobedience, or pride in your life Open your heart to God and pray the prayer David prayed: "Search me, O God, and know my heart: try me, and know my thoughts: and see if there be any wicked way in me, and lead me in the way everlasting" (Ps. 139:23–24). Begin to "humble yourselves therefore under the mighty hand of God, that he may exalt you in due time" (1 Pet. 5:6).

Sometimes the problem is us. We are prideful, rebellious, and unwilling to submit to the authority God has placed in our lives. Instead of humbling ourselves, repenting, and getting deliverance, we blame the pastors, elders, praise and worship team, and the prophetic team. But we rarely look at ourselves and allow God to deal with us and to help us overcome our own issues.

Pride is a common demon. It is just as likely to be found in the ministry as it is in the marketplace. Remember, the Israelites could not go into the Promised Land because they were stiff-necked, stubborn, and disobedient. That whole generation died in the wilderness. When forty years had passed, Joshua and Caleb and the new generation of God's people went in. God does not give His land, His promises to stiff-necked, stubborn, rebellious, hard-hearted, proud, disobedient people. It does not work. It will never work.

In Scripture the land represents the promises and blessing of God, the inheritance of Christ. It is the land of promise, God's promise to you—His vision and dream for your life. It represents abundance, favor, blessing, and prosperity. In the land we worship and we enjoy peace, prosperity, shalom, safety, protection, praise, and glory. All these things are part of the land, and there are many believers who, for different reasons, are not enjoying them.

If you are not a believer, then you have no right to the land. You won't enjoy it. But if you are a believer but are in rebellion and are disobedient to God, you won't get to experience or enjoy the land either. Remember, the Israelites could not go into the land because of rebellion. Isaiah 1:19 says, "If ye be willing and obedient, ye shall eat the good of the land," so there is a level of willingness and obedience required. If you are backslidden and not walking with God, you cannot go into the good land.

Please understand I am not writing this to beat you up. I'm not here to condemn you but to encourage you to get into a place of obedience. Do what God has told you to do if you want to enjoy the good land. You may be wondering why you are not enjoying God's best, and sometimes, if you're honest, you put it on God, saying, "Maybe it's not the will of God for me to have it." Let me assure you: it is the will of God for you to live in the good land, but it is also the will of God for you to be willing and obedient so that you can eat the good of the land.

Take a Self-Inventory

Perhaps you are reading this and the Spirit of God is graciously revealing to you that there are areas of your life where you are in disobedience, sin, or rebellion. Perhaps you are not walking with God the way you know you should be. Even though you are attending church, there are things you are not doing that God told you to do. Perhaps you have not laid aside certain sins and practices, and you are allowing them to keep you away from God's best. God can bring you out of that if you are willing and obedient. He will cause you to eat of the good of the land.

You need to come out of Egypt. You can't get into the good land if you're still in bondage. Your freedom begins with salvation and deliverance. Just as the Israelites went into the wilderness, you will be led there as well—for a short period of time—as God purges you, delivers you, and sets you free. The wilderness place is only temporary. It is never the will of God for His people to stay in the wilderness for years and years. It is the will of God for you to come out of sin, out of Egypt, and through the Red Sea, the waters of baptism, to be baptized in the cloud and in the sea (the people of Israel crossed the Red Sea). Even in their exodus story we see types and shadows of baptism of water and of the Holy Spirit.

God will bring you to the mountain and give you His word. Of course, when you go into the land, some clearing of the land needs to take place. That is still deliverance or spiritual warfare, as you are driving out the evil spirits. His Spirit will guide you through this, but again, only if you are willing and obedient.

You have seen what will keep you from possessing the land. Now I want you to take inventory of your life. If you see that you are not possessing the good land—a place of peace, prosperity, health and wholeness, goodness, fruitfulness and abundance, and so on—which of the ten keys mentioned earlier are you not displaying? If you find yourself angry, bitter, fretful, not trusting in God, proud, unteachable, or doing things your own way, then you will not inherit the land. But if you repent and follow the ten keys, God will exalt you in due season and bring you into the land that flows with milk and honey.

Furthermore, if you are not entering into the promises of God after years and years of confession, praying, shouting, and dancing, you need to take an inventory of your life. Ask yourself the following questions:

- Is there any pride in my life?
- Do I get angry when I get corrected?
- Is there an area in my life where I am not obeying God?
- Do I talk about my supervisors or church leadership?
- Do I hate my bosses or the leaders in my church?
- Do I criticize authority in various areas of my life?
- Do I always have a problem with leadership?
- Do I run from church to church?
- Am I double-minded?
- Do I operate in rejection and rebellion?

These are things that can prevent you from entering into the fullness of God's promises. Isaiah 1:19–20 says, "If ye be willing and obedient, ye shall eat the good of the land: but if ye refuse and rebel, ye shall be devoured with the sword: for the mouth of the Lord hath spoken it." Life, ministry, family, finances, health—you cannot enter into the promises of God in any of these areas without being meek and humble. It will not happen, because God resists the proud.

It's OK to take inventory of your life. We all have to do it from time to time. It is important to realize that everybody is not wrong about us. We may call them haters, but everybody is not lying. Some criticisms are valid. I include myself in this. Every criticism is not given out of hatred or jealousy. Yes, I know there is a thing called a critical spirit and some of the things people say are a result of their jealousy or envy—I believe that—but everyone is not lying or wrong.

Consider the words of those who are closest to you and love you, those who tell you the truth. Do you have trouble receiving what they say as well? There are things that we can't see about ourselves that others can. So while you want to be careful who you listen to, remember that everything is not sent from the enemy to make you feel guilty or accused. There is no condemnation for those who are in Christ, but it is the grace and mercy and love of God that chastens us, and sometimes that chastening comes by way of those who love us enough to tell us the truth. Let the Spirit of God lead you into all truth, which sets you free, taking these matters before the Lord and not being so quick to deny what is being said.

God desires that you be free. He wants the best for you. And He absolutely wants you to be able to enjoy the good land. But He doesn't bless mess. You are called to adhere to God's standard of holiness and righteousness as you grow in Christ. Otherwise you will be one of the rebellious who dwell in a dry land. The good land does not agree with rebellion and pride. It will not cooperate with you. It will not yield its fruit or increase to you. Canaan did not support the pride and rebellion of Israel. They were put out and delivered into Babylonian captivity. We also see this in the fall of Adam and Eve; they were expelled from the Garden of Eden because of disobedience.

We must renounce these spirits from controlling our lives and determining our future in God. If we want to dwell in the good land, we must break free from rebellion, pride, bitterness, and disobedience. We must repent, get deliverance, and fall out of agreement with the enemy so that we can live a lifestyle of grace and humility.

Chapter 2

COMING INTO GOD'S BEST

BEFORE WE GO to the next chapter and learn how to leave the Lots behind, I want you to understand how important it is to prepare yourself to receive the best that God has to offer you. If you don't know that God has His best in mind for you, if you don't have faith that what is for you is for you and that you must remain focused and pursue it regardless of the naysayers, you will continue to wander around in the wilderness. You must get it in your spirit that the good land is God's best and it is God's will for you to have it.

Many of us have been taught that we shouldn't expect or want the best, that we shouldn't think of ourselves worthy enough to be the best or go after it. This is not God's plan for you. He delights in the prosperity of His servants (Ps. 35:27). Evangelist Andrew Wommack summarized my thoughts on this when he said the following:

> The main reason we aren't receiving His best is because we are willing to settle for less. Very few are committed to God's best. We have been influenced more by the world than by God's Word and "dumbed down" to accept far less than what God has provided. As long as you can live with less than God's best, you will.[1]

We need to learn how to receive God's best.

I've flown around the country or around the world many times throughout my life, and sometimes during the flights I'd find myself picking up one airline magazine or another. Though I don't remember which magazine it was from, there was one article I enjoyed reading called "The Best of the Best." The article would rank the best hotels, spas, restaurants, and cruises available at the time.

One thing I realized from this article is that people recognize the best. There are awards for best songs, best movies, best artists, best actors, best athletes, best teachers, and best chefs. There is a list of best places to live, best places to visit, best places to vacation, and best places to do business. Champions are considered the best in their sport. Everyone should strive to be the best at what they do. And like a champion, you should always give your best effort at any endeavor you take on.

People come for counsel because they want to know the best course of action. We all want to make the best decisions in life. We want to marry the best person. We want our families and children to be the best. No one wants the worst. People try their best to avoid the worst.

When people don't feel they have the best, they often pledge to do better. Things that are not the best are in need of improvement or an upgrade. The same is true for us when we are not up to par. We are always striving to be the best and do the best. "And why?" Psalm 95:3–5 says, "Because GOD is the best, High King over all the gods. In one hand he holds deep caves and caverns, in the other hand grasps the high mountains. He made Ocean—he owns it! His hands sculpted Earth!" (MSG).

God, of course, is the best. He is the highest and most excellent. He is the best in love, mercy, grace, holiness, and compassion. God is not only the best, but He also gives the best. God wants you to have the best.

I prophesied one Sunday that we would enter a season of God's best, which goes hand in hand with the revelation of our entering into a good land. The verse the Lord gave me concerning this was Psalm 147:14, "He maketh peace in thy borders, and filleth thee with the finest of the wheat." The best is the finest. The New Life Version translates this verse, "He makes peace within your walls. He fills you with the best grain."

As I conducted a word study for the word *best*, I discovered synonyms such as "finest, greatest, top, foremost, leading, preeminent, premier, prime, first, chief, principal, supreme, of the highest quality, superlative, par excellence, unrivaled, second to none, without equal...peerless, matchless...optimal...ideal...highest, record breaking."[2]

Best in Hebrew is *heleb* or *cheleb*. It comes "from an unused root meaning to be fat; fat, whether literally or figuratively; hence, the richest or choice part:—best, fat(-ness), finest, grease, marrow"; "choicest, best part, abundance (of products of the land)."[3]

According to Sam Oluwatoki:

> The phrase "finest of wheat" [from Psalm 147:14, which I quoted above] implies there are at least three types of fine wheat and the "finest of wheat" being the best of the three i.e. the best of the best. The Psalmist, in our memory verse, reveals God's intention to give His children the best of the best wheat (blessings).[4]

Barnes' Notes says this:

> With the finest of the wheat—Margin, as in Hebrew, with the fat of wheat. The meaning is, the best of the wheat—as the words fat and fatness are often used to denote excellence and abundance. Genesis 27:28, Genesis 27:39; Job 36:16; Psalm 36:8; Psalm 63:5; Psalm 65:11.[5]

I want to challenge you, with these new insights, to begin to believe and confess that you will enjoy the finest. Believe for God's best in your life. Believe for the best doors, the best relationships, the best finances, the best promotions, the best blessings, the best favor, the best increase, the best breakthroughs, the best insight, the best vision, the best praise, the best worship, the best harvest, the best land, and the best ideas.

As Pastor Rich Doebler once preached, "If we remain sinful, selfish, fearful, bitter, vindictive, suspicious people, we'll never be able to trust God for better things. So first we need a powerful, supernatural work of transformation, which comes through the cross of Jesus Christ. His sacrifice makes it possible for us to live."[6] Because of Jesus' sacrifice we can live as though we believe Jesus gives us the best. He even made a statement about His giving the best in His first public miracle, when He turned water into wine at the wedding at Cana.

> And said to him, "People always serve the best wine first. Later, when the guests are drunk, they serve the cheaper wine. But you have saved the best wine until now."
>
> —JOHN 2:10, ERV

The Expanded Bible translation says this:

> And said to him, "People always serve the best [expensive] wine first. Later, after the guests have been drinking awhile [and are less discriminating], they serve the cheaper [inferior] wine. But you have saved the best [expensive] wine till now."
>
> —JOHN 2:10, EXB

A few verses earlier we see where Mary, Jesus' mother, told Jesus that they had run out of wine. Jesus answered, "Why do you involve me?...My hour has not yet come" (John 2:4, NIV). It seems that Mary ignored Him and told the servants to do whatever He told them to do. The Bible says, "They did so" (v. 8, NIV). And here we see that one way to begin to walk in God's best is to do what He says to do—be obedient.

The best tends to be more expensive because it is of better quality. The inferior is usually less expensive and of a lower quality. Jesus can turn your water into wine. He can transform what is normal into the best. This can happen if you do what He says.

Becoming the Best

Another key to experiencing and becoming the best is virtue. If you recall from the word study above, best is related to excellence. The virtuous woman from Proverbs 31 is the personification of excellence in that she excels them all. She is the best.

> Many daughters have done virtuously, but thou excellest them all.
>
> —PROVERBS 31:29

Virtue will allow you to obtain the best name and reputation (Prov. 22:1). *Virtue* is "goodness, virtuousness, righteousness, morality...integrity, dignity, rectitude...honor...decency, respectability, nobility...worthiness...purity."[7]

It is important to be the best in your character. God took note of Job, who was perfect and upright. There was no one in his generation more righteous. He was the best man of his generation. The righteous have the highest and best standards.

Israel had the best laws of any nation. God expected them to be the best in keeping them. The nations would recognize their greatness, laws, and wisdom (Deut. 4:6).

God promised to make His people the best. They would be the head and not the tail. They would lend and not borrow. They would be blessed in the city and in the field. They would come into the best land that produced the best harvest and provided for them the best life, safe from all enemies. This was and still is God's plan for His people today.

Desire the Best Gifts

> But covet earnestly the best gifts: and yet shew I unto you a more excellent way.
>
> —1 Corinthians 12:31

Prophecy is one of the best gifts. Prophecy does so much for the believer. Prophecy edifies, exhorts, comforts, heals, delivers, refreshes, confirms, gives life, builds, plants, gives courage, directs, reveals, activates, and imparts. The prophetic life is one of the best you can live. You hear God's voice and rely on His word and purposes.

Wisdom is another of God's best gifts. Wisdom will deliver to you the best. Wisdom speaks excellent (the best) things.

> Hear; for I will speak of *excellent* things; and the opening of my lips shall be right things.
>
> —Proverbs 8:6, emphasis added

Excellence is the highest, the best. A life of wisdom is the best life. Wisdom helps you make the best decisions. Wisdom helps you receive the best counsel. Wisdom gives you the best understanding.

Receiving God's Best

When it comes to receiving God's best, the first thing we should set our minds toward is to not accept less than God's best as we discussed above. The next thing is to give back to God our best, including our best sacrifices and offerings.

> All the best of the oil, and all the best of the wine, and of
> the wheat, the firstfruits of them which they shall offer
> unto the LORD, them have I given thee.
>
> —NUMBERS 18:12

God honors our sacrifice when it is our best.

> The best I have to bring, I'll throw it all into the fire as
> the fragrance of my sacrifice ascends unto you. *Pause in
> his presence.*
>
> —PSALM 66:15, TPT

In the good land there is a path that leads to the best. Then
there is a river that takes you to the best gold.

> And the gold of that land is the best, and there is found
> bdellium, that is, a tree of spicery, and the stone onyx;
> (and the gold of that land is the best, and bdellium, that
> is, a spice tree, is also found there, and the onyx stone
> as well).
>
> —GENESIS 2:12, WYC

The final two keys to receiving God's best—listening to
God and walking in His ways—lead me to point out why
many of us do not receive God's best.

Why we don't receive God's best

There are two verses in the King James Version that mention
"the finest of the wheat"—Psalm 147:14 and Psalm 81:16—and
we know from the word study above that *finest* also means "best."
Psalm 81 gives the reason why people don't receive and walk in
God's best.

> Oh that my people had hearkened unto me, and Israel
> had walked in my ways! I should soon have subdued
> their enemies, and turned my hand against their adver-
> saries. The haters of the LORD should have submitted
> themselves unto him: but their time should have endured

for ever. He should have fed them also with the finest of the wheat: and with honey out of the rock should I have satisfied thee.

—PSALM 81:13–16

In order to live in God's best, we must listen to and obey the voice of God and follow His direction. We must walk in the ways of God. We come to Zion, a type of the kingdom and of the good land, to learn God's ways (Isa. 2:3). The ways of God include love, mercy, truth, righteousness, forgiveness, holiness, and faith. God will teach us His ways (Ps. 86:11; 143:8).

Oh, dear people, will you listen to me now? Israel, will you follow my map? I'll make short work of your enemies, give your foes the back of my hand. I'll send the GOD-haters cringing like dogs, never to be heard from again. You'll feast on my fresh-baked bread spread with butter and rock-pure honey.

—PSALM 81:13–16, MSG

The Amplified version says, "Oh, that My people would listen to Me, that Israel would walk in My ways!" Wisdom warns those who will not listen to Him.

Calamity, fear, destruction, and desolation are the opposite of the best.

But ye have set at nought all my counsel, and would none of my reproof: I also will laugh at your calamity; I will mock when your fear cometh; when your fear cometh as desolation, and your destruction cometh as a whirlwind; when distress and anguish cometh upon you.

—PROVERBS 1:25–27

When you reject wisdom, wisdom will reject you. You cannot have the best without the help of wisdom, if you despise and turn your back on wisdom. The fear of the Lord is the beginning of wisdom (Prov. 9:10). The fear of the Lord is therefore a key to enjoying God's best. When we fear the Lord, we revere, trust, and take seriously the benefits of obeying Him.

When we fear Him, God will cause us to hear His voice, and direct us in the right way—the way in which we should go. Isaiah gives us a powerful promise:

> And thine ears shall hear a word behind thee, saying, This is the way, walk ye in it, when ye turn to the right hand, and when ye turn to the left.
>
> —ISAIAH 30:21

You can trust God to speak to you and lead you. God will lead you to the best. The Book of Deuteronomy gives another promise to those who walk in God's ways:

> The LORD shall command the blessing upon thee in thy storehouses, and in all that thou settest thine hand unto; and he shall bless thee in the land which the LORD thy God giveth thee. The LORD shall establish thee an holy people unto himself, as he hath sworn unto thee, if thou shalt keep the commandments of the LORD thy God, and walk in his ways. And all people of the earth shall see that thou art called by the name of the LORD; and they shall be afraid of thee.
>
> —DEUTERONOMY 28:8–10

God commands His blessing upon your life. God commands the best for your life. God commands His blessing on your storehouses. Others will respect and fear you.

A word to backsliders

Return to God and receive the best. The prodigal son received the best robe.

> But the father said to his servants, Bring forth the best robe, and put it on him; and put a ring on his hand, and shoes on his feet.
>
> —Luke 15:22

The prodigal son was not living his best life. He spent all his money on riotous living and found himself in the pigpen. But when he came to himself and returned home, his father received him and welcomed him with the best. He threw his son the best party and killed the best calf. When we've gone off to a far country spiritually, we too can come back and be welcomed into the best in our Father's house.

Favor and God's best

Favor will take you to the best place. Though Esther was taken from her home and put into a life she did not want, we can trace God's favor over her life as He provided her with the best place among the other women. She received His best protection and wisdom to bring deliverance to her people. Just as Esther received favor for God's best (Esther 2:15, 17), you can be favored with the best.

> And the maiden pleased him, and she obtained kindness of him; and he speedily gave her her things for purification, with such things as belonged to her, and seven maidens, which were meet to be given her, out of the king's house: and he preferred her and her maids unto the best place of the house of the women.
>
> —Esther 2:9

Esther and her maidens were taken to the best place. They had the best rooms. The Living Bible says, "the most luxurious apartment." Wisdom also delivers favor (Prov. 3:4; 8:35). Those who are favored receive the best.

Joseph Prince pointed out the following:

[Esther] did not trust in her own efforts. While the women tried to outdo one another by relying on their own efforts, Esther wisely submitted to the one person who would know the king's preferences best, and the results speak for themselves....Esther depended entirely upon the Lord's unmerited favor....Esther did not have to struggle. When she rested in the Lord and humbled herself, the Lord promoted her and exalted her above all the other beautiful women. God resists the proud and gives unmerited faith to the humble (1 Peter 5:5).[8]

Chapter 3

LEAVING LOT

THE STORY OF Lot and Abraham (then named Abram) is a familiar one. If you've read this account, then you may have noted that God called Abraham out from among his family but didn't necessarily call Lot. Yet Abraham allowed Lot to come with him as he set out to follow God to a new and unknown land. (See Genesis 12:1–5.) Upon Abraham and Lot's arrival in the land that God had shown Abraham, strife erupted between their camps (Gen. 13:7). The Bible says that "the land was not able to bear them, that they might dwell together" (v. 6), so Abraham said to Lot, "Let there be no strife...separate thyself, I pray thee, from me: if thou wilt take the left hand, then I will go to the right; or if thou depart to the right hand, then I will go to the left" (vv. 8–9).

There comes a point in our journey to the good land, and even as we cross over into what God has promised us, that we must separate from some people. This is not easy. We may have deep love for some of the people. We may go way back, but in order to move forward, we may have to leave some behind. Many of them may mean well, but they are carrying beliefs about us, God, and themselves that will hold us back from experiencing the fullness of God's promises. So in this chapter

I'm going to talk about the importance of getting every Lot out of your life.

Lot is an individual, and Lot is also a spirit that will cause you not to inherit and enjoy the land that God has for you. At some point or another we are all challenged with a Lot in our lives, no matter who we are. And it is important that we learn how to separate from them so that we can enjoy the good land.

Separate From Strife and Contention

If you're going into the good land, you have to leave the land you are in. This doesn't mean you have to move geographically, like Abraham did, though that might be possible. Typically the move to the good land is a change of spiritual residence, a change of spiritual address.

You cannot stay in the old place and enjoy the good land. God is calling you to migrate out of the old and into the new. Abraham was called out of Ur, the land of the Chaldeans, and told to go to a land of promise. He obeyed God and began to move, even though he didn't know where he was going. It was a walk of faith.

But then Abraham had his nephew, Lot, with him. Sometimes family wants to follow as we migrate from the old place to the new one, and sometimes family can be the biggest hindrance to your enjoying the land. In Abraham and Lot's case, when they got to the land God showed Abraham, they began to grow, and there was strife between Abraham's herdsmen and Lot's herdsmen over water. They began to argue and fight. So Abraham went to his nephew and said, "Look. This is not going to work. We can't have strife, fighting, and arguing in this land." He told Lot to choose: "Where are you going to go?"

Lot chose the plane of Sodom, which at that time was a very fertile plane. (This is another whole story.) So they separated there.

If you're going to enjoy the land, you must get the Lots out of your life. Lot represents strife and contention. If there is any person bringing strife, contention, arguing, or fighting into your life and your land, that relationship is not worth holding on to, because strife will destroy the peace and prosperity you hope to enjoy in the good land.

I am by no means saying you can just leave your husband or wife. I'm talking about relationships in general. Marriage is a covenant, so if you are having marriage problems, if you are fighting and arguing, get counseling or deliverance and resolve those issues. There are, however, relationships with people you are connected to who come with their baggage, with strife and arguing, and it is not worth losing the blessing and promise that God has for you by trying to maintain the connection.

Abraham separated from Lot because he knew that as long as they were together, their herdsmen were going to be in conflict. Abraham knew that was not what God called him to. God did not call him out of Ur and into the land of promise for him to be involved in strife and division. That is not the promise of God.

Strife is deadly. It causes you to lose your peace. Fighting, arguing, contention, gossiping, backbiting—these are things you should not tolerate in your life. God never intended for you to live a life full of strife, pressure, and confusion, one where you have no peace and no joy. God wants you to enjoy life.

Sometimes we have to separate. We have to get the Lots out of our lives. Remember, the good land is a land of shalom. The word *shalom* means peace, prosperity, wholeness, health, healing, and so much more. The good land is a land of peace. God expects you to enjoy the fullness of shalom in the land.

Everywhere you look—even in church, among Christians, and on social media—people are arguing and fighting over posts, over churches and ministries. Before you know it, you're in arguments with people. You're in strife. You're angry. You end up using all kinds of unclean and foul language. That is not the good land. That is not what God called you to. That is the spirit of Lot in your life, and it is an assignment of hell. Sometimes it's a person very close to you who brings strife and contention into your life and causes you to lose your peace, your shalom. Lot was Abraham's nephew. You can't enjoy the land as long as Lot is there.

Level With Lot

In following Abraham's example, in order to get the Lots out of your life, talk to them. Tell them, "I cannot be in this relationship any longer because there is too much contention, strife, and division. You go your way. I'll go mine. No hard feelings."

Again, I'm not referring to marriage, so please don't take this as a prophetic word for you to divorce your mate or leave your husband. That's another subject. I'm referring to other relationship we are in that are holding us back from the new places God wants to take us.

Sometimes in the church, the house of God, or on the job you have to level with the Lots and cut ties. You may need to say, "I will not allow strife and division in my land. I will not allow contention, arguing, and fighting in my land. I will not allow gossip, backbiting, profanity, anger, and hatred in my land. These things cannot dwell with me. My land is meant to be a place of shalom, peace, prosperity, and abundance. I cannot and will not allow myself to operate in a place of strife and contention. I will not allow it."

Once you get Lot away, you can then step into the promise and blessing of God. You are able to get into the land of promise and enjoy the land. God never intended for you to live a life full of pain, grief, sorrow, and sadness where you are vexed, can't sleep, and your blood pressure is going up. Strife is one of the worst things that can happen to us as believers, when the peace or shalom of God is our portion. Some people love mess. They love arguing, fighting, and contention. But that is not the good land.

Even in my own life I have committed to not allow people to pull me out of the land of promise, the land of blessing, joy, and peace that God has for me. I am committed to remove every Lot from my life. If you are a Lot and have attached yourself to me, if you have come into the land with me and are causing strife between us, we have to separate. We will not argue and fight over land. God called me out of my land and told me to come into this new land. He didn't call me to have an issue with you and yours. There's plenty good land for both you and me.

The decision to get rid of Lot is yours. It is not God's. Abraham had to obey God and leave the land where he lived to migrate to the new land. Sometimes we leave it up to God, saying, "Well, God, if You want me to enjoy this land, then You should just give it to me." God will give you the land, but you have to make some decisions. You have to obey the word of the Lord.

How we experience the manifestation of the good land is based on our choices. We do not have to settle for anything less. A lot of believers settle for living in the wilderness, living in Egypt, living in a dry place, and living with Lots, saying, "Well, it must just be the will of God for me not to be blessed and not to prosper. I guess I'll see all this when I get to heaven." No. God wants you to enjoy this life now, and a part of that is revelation, understanding the decisions you can make to take hold of what God has for you.

A Place Better Than Where You've Been

When I got saved, I lost all my friends. All my drug buddies left me. They laughed at me when I spoke in tongues and went to church. They thought I had lost my mind. Although really, they didn't leave me; I started going in a different direction.

Some time ago I went back to that part of town for a funeral. I hadn't seen many of the people there for forty years. The choices some of them made with their lives did not turn out well for them. Seeing them after such a long time helped me see how the grace of God covers us even in aging. Some who had made decisions to stay in bad situations, in addictions, and in the dry land looked twice their age. Others looked like they had done well for themselves.

I believe that bitterness, anger, rebellion, and disobedience can put a whipping on you. People who are thirty and forty will end up looking like they are seventy. But the glory of God, being filled with the Holy Ghost, can beautify you. People will wonder how it is that you have been able to maintain so well for so long. This is what a good life in the good land can do for you.

You do not have to stay in a dry, depressing, and stressful place. You can come out of a place—the hood or other bad circumstance—and determine that you don't want to live like that anymore, while still having love for the people there. You are not wrong for believing that God has more for you, that you don't have to live in a low place, that there is a bigger land prepared for you, and that you can step up into a prosperous and blessed place. You can boldly declare, "I am going to walk in abundance. I am going to enjoy joy and peace. I am going to experience the good things in life. I am not going to struggle all of my life. I'm not going to make excuses because I was born a certain way or into a certain neighborhood."

God will save you, deliver you, bless you, and promote you, but you have to obey Him and leave Lot and the old land behind. Don't be like those who never walk in the good land because they never leave the old.

Your old land could be some religious church that doesn't embrace anything new—no new revelation, no new unction. Same old songs, same old people, same old traditions, same old messages—nothing new, nothing fresh. Then as you grow in God and learn about how big He is, you learn about the prophetic and deliverance—but they refuse it. They keep the same five people singing in the choir, and they want you to just sit there. Then when you go visit another church, they want to know what you were doing over there.

Your response: "Brother, I'm looking for the good land. This is not it. This is the dry land."

But so many people sit right in those dead churches, saying, "This is where I grew up. My momma and daddy went here. My grandparents went here. This has been my church all my life. I am waiting on God to move me." And they will sit right there until they die.

Don't be like that. Be strong and courageous. Pursue the leading of God. Answer when He calls. Be brave and step out into the new thing in faith. People may look at you like you are crazy. They are not bad people. They may love you; you may love them. But they are stuck. Don't let their "stuckness" temper your pursuit. Launch out into the new. You and God search for a church with new messages, new ministries, and new vision. Look for a new land, a good land. Come out of tradition.

You have the sense that there is something more and better for you—and you are not wrong. There is another place for you. You will not remain stuck there selling one more chicken or fish dinner. You will not be relegated to participating in one more rummage sale, raffle, pastor's anniversary, or founders' meeting. You will answer God's call to go to a new land that He will show you.

A Walk of Faith

Journeying into the good land is a walk of faith. You have to step out in faith and do what you've never done before. You may not know exactly where you are going, but the Spirit stirs you, and you know you must get out of wherever you are. The feeling can be so strong that you catch yourself thinking or saying, "I'm out of here, even if I die on my way to the good land. I'd rather die on the way than to die in this place. I'm dying anyway; I might as well die on my way. I don't know where I'm going, but I know it's better than where I am right now."

Someone may ask you, "Where are you going?"

For the moment you may respond with "I have no idea, but I am out of here."

"You can't just go to a place you don't know," they might respond.

"Yes I can. God is with me. I'm out of here. Wherever I am supposed to be, I know this is not it. This is bad. Nothing is growing here."

Dead things. Dead places. Buzzards flying around.

I once went to a church in Minnesota. The pastor had asked me to come and minister to his people and to pray because his church wasn't growing. It was the winter, and when he turned the heat on, bats started flying out of the vents. I said, "This is why your church isn't growing. We don't do bats."

Moving into the good land is a faith walk. It's about obeying God. When God tells you to move, you shift. When God says there is something better, you step out in faith. You do it. You obey God. Psalm 37 says that if we are meek, if we trust in the Lord and wait patiently for Him, He will give us the land as an inheritance. He will bring it to pass.

My Experience With Lot

When I made a decision as a minister to live in the good land, I began to step into some new things in my own life—financially, spiritually, and influentially. Some people who had gotten used to me at a certain level got upset. In an effort to bring them into the land with me, I purposed to minister to some of them in every way I knew how, but they did not want to go forward. Strife and contention began to seep into the camp. But I was determined to move forward into what God had for me and leave their opinions and issues with them and God, still caring for them in ministry as I could while remaining faithful in the new things God was bringing into my life.

People have beliefs about ministers and prosperity, promotion, and being sought after. As long as pastors and leaders are struggling, the church members pray for them. When they start to break through, the people get upset. They have a problem.

Let me say this: Pastors believe God just like you do. We're believing God for things just like you are. People get upset with pastors when they begin to step into new things—new relationships, new circles, new realms of authority, and so forth. Many people want their pastor to stay in the same place. But God wants to move us all into a good land—both you and your pastor. If you aren't ready to go, don't hold your pastor back or begrudge him or her of the blessings he or she begins to receive.

And to you, pastor, leader, minister, or lay person: there are some people you can't take with you into the good land. They are not ready to go, and you must move on without them. You love them and you bless them, but you can't take them with you. They are not ready, because their minds can't envision anything beyond where they currently are. Some may get jealous or envious and begin to talk about you, but keep pursuing the place God has for you. Level with them and say,

"God has blessed me to come out of the old and step into the new. And God will do the same thing for you." They only need to make a decision that there is a land for them too. God has something for you and for them. You are children of God.

See Beyond the Natural Land

> By faith Abraham obeyed when he was called to go out
> to the place which he would receive as an inheritance.
> And he went out, not knowing where he was going. By
> faith he dwelt in the land of promise as in a foreign
> country, dwelling in tents with Isaac and Jacob, the heirs
> with him of the same promise; for he waited for the city
> which has foundations, whose builder and maker is God.
> —HEBREWS 11:8–10, NKJV

We know Abraham took a leap of faith and obeyed God. He left his country and went to the land God showed him, which was the land of Canaan. But Hebrews 11 gives us a picture that Abraham was looking beyond this natural land, beyond this earthly place God had led him to and looked toward a "city which has foundations, whose builder and maker is God." We know this city to be Zion.

As I have been sharing, the land of Israel, the city of Jerusalem, the temple system was only a type, a shadow, something temporary, something physical that was to be replaced by something greater. The earthly was only a picture or a type of the heavenly. So there was an earthly Zion, or Jerusalem, but we know there is also a heavenly Zion, a heavenly Jerusalem.

In Hebrews 12:22 the writer says, "You have come to Mount Zion and to the city of the living God, the heavenly Jerusalem" (NKJV). Then in Revelation 21 John sees this heavenly Jerusalem coming down from heaven. It has twelve gates, three on each side—east, west, north, and south. And the nations come and bring their glory and honor to it. It's heavenly. It's spiritual. It is not an earthly city but something that is much greater.

When we talk about the good land today, it can refer to something physical. With promises such as "the righteous shall inherit the land" and "the meek shall inherit the earth," you can believe God for physical, natural land—and depending on God's call on your life, believing this is important. God will give you land and property. People who have begun to grasp this message have already told me testimonies of receiving land or property for their businesses, homes, and other types of real estate. So you can claim the promises based around the good land for the physical needs or desires you have. Psalm 37 talks about the righteous inheriting land. When I drive through a city and see vacant land, I always stretched my hand toward it and say, "Lord, let the righteous inherit the land. Let the people of God inherit the land." But what I want to get you to see is that there's something much greater than the physical.

Abraham looked for a city with foundations, whose builder and maker is God (Heb. 11:10). He looked for a city that was not built by man. He looked for a city that is not earthly. He looked for something beyond the natural. It's the city we come to when we accept Christ. We come to Zion; we come to the heavenly city. We are born of this city. We are born from above. We are citizens of Zion, and we approach and come into this city.

This place is the good land. It's a place of worship and glory. It is the mountain of God. It's the river of God. It's a place of dominion, power, and revelation. It's a high place. It's a place of God's presence and glory. It's living in the power and anointing of God, the blessings and rain of heaven. It's a place where the river of God flows out of your belly. As Jesus said, "Out of [your] belly shall flow rivers of living water" (John 7:38). It's life in the Spirit. It's joy. It's peace. It's Spirit-filled living. It's enjoying God. It's enjoying His presence. It's enjoying His city and His land. It's what Abraham saw—something beyond the natural, something we have in Christ.

> For the kingdom of God is not eating and drinking, but righteousness and peace and joy in the Holy Spirit.
> —ROMANS 14:17, NKJV

Again, Abraham was looking for something beyond this natural land—a city with foundations, whose builder and maker is God (Heb. 11:10). What a powerful verse of Scripture to tell us that Abraham saw something beyond the natural. Because remember, at this point in the narrative, Abraham would die, and his descendants would not come into the land until after four hundred years. They would first be in bondage in Egypt, and God would bring them out of Egypt and into the land of Canaan. They would enjoy the physical land one day, but not yet. It was only a type, a picture of something much greater that we have in Christ.

God revealed to Abraham that there is something even bigger—a city that He built, a city that has a foundation—Zion. And by faith Abraham lived in this land of promise, yet still he looked beyond it. He was seeing something greater. This is what God wants you to see. He wants you to see the greater.

While many people focus on earthly Jerusalem, there's something greater than that. I keep saying this over and over again because it is really strong in the church today. Everybody looks at Jerusalem, saying, "That's the holy city," but Messiah came to raise up a new group of people, a new nation called the church who occupy a heavenly kingdom, a heavenly Jerusalem.

The writer of Hebrews 12:22 was telling the Hebrews who were connected to the old city, connected to earthly Jerusalem, that they had come to Mount Zion, the greater Jerusalem. What a word! This means that now the greater is come. You don't need the old. You don't walk in the old covenant. You don't live under that. The old system has been done away with. What a blessing to live in liberty and freedom and to live beyond the natural.

Don't be confused when it comes to Jerusalem. There are two Jerusalems in Scripture: the earthly and the heavenly. There's the natural, then there's the spiritual. Why do people focus on the earthly and the natural when they have the greater?

So often people want to go back. They become their own Lots in some cases, allowing themselves to go only so far with God. But God doesn't want us to go back. We move forward. We move to the heavenly and we enjoy it. We enjoy the rain from heaven, the blessing of heaven, the river of God, the Spirit of God, the move of God, revival, glory, praise, and worship. We enjoy God's presence. We enjoy peace, shalom, health, healing, prosperity, deliverance, and joy. The joy of the Lord is our strength. We enjoy financial prosperity as well. That comes as a result, but the kingdom of God does not come with observation (Luke 17:20). Luke 17:21 says, "Neither shall [men] say, Lo here! or, lo there! for, behold, the kingdom of God is within you." It's inward. It's spiritual. It's heavenly. It's by the Spirit of God—not by might, not by power, but by His Spirit.

This is why I love worship and why I talk so much about the worshipping prophet Asaph and glory. That is the good land. Revelation 21 talks about the heavenly city of God, which is full of God's glory. This city does not need the light of the sun or the moon because the Lamb is the light of it (v. 23). It is full of God's glory. It is the glory realm, the realm of the presence of God. That's the realm you live in. You don't just come in and out of God's presence. You are a citizen of Zion. You enjoy God's presence every day. New favor, new grace, new glory, new mercies are upon you every day. You enjoy the river of God every day.

The Good Land Is Kingdom Normal

The good land is a lifestyle. It is what I call "kingdom normal." Encountering the glory of God should be normal. It should be something you experience on a consistent basis. We go around the country doing glory gatherings, and many people come and say they've never before experienced anything like the prophetic worship or the glory of God. I tell them this is kingdom normal. This is what you should be enjoying all the time. But sometimes we go to places where the emphasis is not the glory of God—not worship, the prophetic, or the river of God—due to a lack of revelation, a lack of teaching, and a lack of faith in this area. No teaching and no revelation. What should be normal, isn't.

When you grow up in a city, the things you encounter in everyday life in that city should be normal. That is your lifestyle, the normal atmosphere, whether you're from New York, Chicago, Los Angeles, or Miami. You don't wake up every day and say, "Oh my goodness, look at this city." No; it becomes normal to you. The same is true of the heavenly. It becomes normal. Revelation, dreams, visions, prophecy, tongues, interpretation, healings, miracles, faith, discerning of spirits, word of knowledge, word of wisdom, breakthroughs, signs, wonders, presence, glory, vowing, songs of the Lord, minstrels, new sounds, blessings, favor, rain—all this is normal. This is kingdom normal. This is the heavenly. Even though we're living on the earth, we enjoy the heavenly.

Believe God and begin to confess the things God is revealing to you concerning the good land. Begin to decree and believe them, because they are your inheritance. The righteous shall inherit the land. The meek shall inherit the earth. But again, it's something greater than the physical. It's your inheritance. It is what belongs to you in Christ. Don't let tradition, religion, or any Lots steal your inheritance away from you. No. Possess it. It is yours in Christ. And by faith you can walk in it.

I believe that as you hear this word, faith is being stirred in your heart. As you study it, you will get a revelation of it and begin to walk in it. You will begin to enjoy the good land. You will begin to enjoy the heavenly city. You will begin to enjoy Zion. Your life will change. You will come out of the old and go into the new. You are a new creature in God, a new creation. You are filled with new wine. God has given you a new commandment, a new covenant, a new heaven, and a new earth. He makes all things new. The good land is yours. Enjoy it. Don't let religion, bondage, or preachers mess it up for you. Don't live under condemnation, guilt, shame, the law, legalism, bondage, joylessness, control, witchcraft, manipulation, domination, religion, and tradition, with no praise, no worship, no glory, and no presence. Don't get stuck in these old religious systems. Get out. Find a church full of glory. Find a church that is full of worship and revelation, one that embraces the prophetic, deliverance, and the power of God. I don't care if you have to drive an hour to get there. Some people drive three or four hours to get to Crusaders Church because they want to be around the heavenly realm.

Don't dry up and die in a place that has no revelation, teaching, prophecy, deliverance, presence, glory, song of the Lord, or Zion. It doesn't matter what Lots may want to hang on to you and keep you from moving forward into what God has for you. Even if your mother went there, your dad went there, and you grew up there—if God is calling you to something new, leave. God told Abraham to get out of his country and get into the good land. I encourage you to get into the good land. Embrace it. Get a vision of it. It will change your life.

There is a city that has foundations whose builder and maker is God. It's heavenly. It's good. It's Zion. It's new. It comes down from heaven. It's here now. We enjoy it. We walk in it. We are born in that city, born from above, born again. We are citizens of that city. We come into that place called Zion, the mountain of God; the place of dominion, power, blessing, rain, and refreshing glory. What a lifestyle. What a blessing to live and walk in this realm.

Chapter 4

CLEARING THE LAND

MANY YEARS AGO I did a teaching on deliverance called "Clearing the Land," which was based on the time when the Israelites were crossing over into the land God had promised them. Before the Israelites got there, God told them to drive out the nations that occupied the land upon their arrival—the Canaanites, Hittites, Hivites, and Jebusites. These were unclean nations that were dwelling in the land of Canaan. They were idolaters involved in all kinds of witchcraft, familiar spirits, divination, soothsaying, Baal worship, sexual perversion, temple prostitution, and other types of uncleanness. The Bible says that the land was defiled and that it would vomit or spew out the inhabitants (Lev. 18:25).

Throughout the Book of Joshua we read how God sent the Israelites into the land to drive out their enemies. He told the Israelites to tear down the altars and burn their idols, their graven images. He commanded that they should not even take the gold and silver from the graven images because it was cursed and dedicated to demons. They were commanded to completely purge the land with fire.

Their actions are a type or picture of deliverance, as Jesus, who is the true Israel of God, came out of Egypt and drove the enemy from God's people just as Israel did. As He grew and came upon His time of ministry, Jesus went to the Jordan River to be baptized. He was baptized by John in the water, which is symbolic of Moses taking Israel through the Red Sea. Then the Spirit of God came upon Jesus, which is a picture of Israel being covered by the cloud, which represented God's presence.

Israel was baptized unto Moses in the sea and in the cloud. Jesus was baptized by John in the water, and the Spirit of God came on Him. Jesus went into the wilderness for forty days. Israel was in the wilderness for forty years. While Israel's extended time in the wilderness was a result of their fall to temptation, Jesus did not fail His time of refinement and testing. He overcame the temptation of the devil in the wilderness, returned in the power of the Spirit, and came back over the Jordan.

Israel came over the Jordan into the land and drove out the idolatrous nations. Jesus came back through the Jordan into the land and began to cast out demons. The idolatrous nations at the time of Israel were likened unto demons in the spirit realm. Jesus is the true Israel of God, and those who are in Christ are part of the true Israel of God, as they have been grafted into the seed of Abraham.

As Jesus began to cast out demons and drive them out of people's lives throughout the land of Galilee, He was clearing the spiritual land just as much as Israel cleared the physical land. When you receive deliverance and have demons cast out of your life, you are clearing and cleansing your spiritual land and are setting up your land to be blessed.

Deliverance is such an important ministry. We all need to go through the process of deliverance in order to deal with rejection, hurt, rebellion, pride, lust, witchcraft, uncleanness, bitterness, unforgiveness, anger, rage, infirmity, and generational spirits. Deliverance has been a main focus of my ministry over the last thirty years. Through deliverance your life, mind, body, emotions, and land will be blessed.

Make No Covenants With the Inhabitants

As you come into the good land, spiritual enemies will already be occupying the space God has promised you. Through a number of avenues, such as generational curses or sins, you have come into agreement with them—sometimes unawares. God will lead you to break those agreements.

The enemy will also send spirits to keep you out of the land. God commands you to immediately cast them out and not enter into any covenants with them. He gave this very warning to the people of Israel in Exodus 23:32–33: "Thou shalt make no covenant with them, nor with their gods. They shall not dwell in thy land, lest they make thee sin against me: for if thou serve their gods, it will surely be a snare unto thee." He told them to destroy those enemy nations and drive them out, and if they didn't, those nations would be a snare and a trap to them, thorns in their sides. God said these nations would seduce Israel, pull Israel under them, and lead them astray.

Then in Judges 2 we discover that the Israelites did not obey God. Instead of thoroughly driving all the nations out of the land, they made covenants with some of them:

> I made you to go up out of Egypt, and have brought you unto the land which I sware unto your fathers; and I said, I will never break my covenant with you. And ye shall make no league with the inhabitants of this land; ye shall throw down their altars: but ye have not obeyed my voice.
>
> —Judges 2:1–2

Eventually the Israelites began to worship the very demons that were behind the idols in the nation. As a result, the Israelites were expelled from the land and were led into seventy years of captivity in Babylon.

Sins That Defile the Good Land

The blessing of God cannot come on the land when the land is defiled or unclean. We must get rid of anything that defiles our land. There are certain sins that do defile; God calls them abominations. The more obvious ones are witchcraft, occultism, and divination. They must be expelled from our land. With them dwelling there, we cannot be blessed. Our land cannot be blessed. These anti-God spirits include things such as charismatic, false prophets; any type of Jezebelic control or manipulation; or cults. You cannot have these things operating in your land and be blessed.

Controlling leadership

Controlling leadership is just another form of witchcraft. Your land will not be blessed if you are sitting under a controlling leader. I've done a lot of teaching on controlling, dominating leadership, and it's very prevalent, especially in Pentecostal churches. Now, I believe in submission to godly authority, but I do not believe in controlling, dominating, and manipulating leadership that controls your life.

The Israelites' land was only blessed when they submitted to the Spirit or the rule of God. God was their King and Ruler, and as they would submit to His Word, He would bless their land. But the Israelites came under kings who led them into idolatry and sin. So be very careful what kind of leadership you sit under. Don't sit under false, controlling, abusive, and dominating leadership. Neither your land nor your life will be blessed.

If you find yourself under submission to this kind of leadership, you need to cleanse your land from controlling Jezebelic, dominating, manipulating people. Don't allow them to control, seduce, and manipulate your life. In Pentecostal

Charismatic churches these people may use tongues, prophecy, and preaching to seduce, control, dominate, and manipulate. They will tell you, "Don't think. Just do what I say."

This is not healthy, and this is not God. Leading people in this way does not bring the blessing of God upon the land. It brings a curse. Instead, submit to godly leaders who are not controlling, manipulative, dominating, and abusive. Submit to those who don't beat, abuse, or control you, who don't try to take everything you have. Don't allow them to bring you under their curses by using their position, saying, "I'm an apostle...I'm a prophet...I'm a bishop. You do what I say," and then cursing you when you leave. That is witchcraft. That is not the way to be blessed.

Find a godly leader and pastor who loves God, loves you, teaches you, trains you, and activates you. Don't be fooled, however—there is nothing wrong with godly correction that is done in love. Find a place where liberty and love reign. When the pastor or leader loves you, teaches you, prays for you, ministers to you in love, and is not controlling or abusive, you will be blessed.

Sexual perversion

Sodomites were in the land—temple prostitutes whose behavior and practice were unclean. Get sexual perversion out of your land. Get delivered from lust and uncleanness. You cannot have that in your land or in your life and expect to live in the good land.

Many struggle in this area, but God will deliver. Submit your flesh to the Spirit of God and obey His Word. Be filled with the Holy Ghost and have discipline and self-control so that you may live a lifestyle that is pleasing.

Ungodly soul ties

Break ungodly soul ties and get away from relationships that are not of God. Separate from people who pull you into unclean lifestyles. Don't have unclean soul ties with people you always end up in bed with, people you are not married to. This is not the way to live in the good land.

Don't let people defile your land. Don't let unclean people run your life and be in your life. If they don't want to be clean, perhaps you can minister to them, but only by your being accountable and discerning of what the Spirit of God wants for you. You can't be soul tied to unclean people, those involved in witchcraft, false doctrine, false prophecy, religious spirits, perversion, and uncleanness. You cannot allow those people to defile you. You cannot be tied to people who use profanity and who gossip, criticize, and backbite. Don't allow them to speak all that filth in your ears.

Don't be afraid to walk alone for a period. It's better to be alone and holy than to be soul tied with people who are unclean, because your land is important. It's important that you have a clean and blessed land.

Bitterness

Bitterness is another way the land can be defiled. Hebrews 12:14–15 tells us, "Follow peace with all men...lest any root of bitterness springing up trouble you, and thereby many be defiled." Bitterness and unforgiveness can defile your land. You cannot live in the good land with bitterness, unforgiveness, anger, hatred, and rage in your life. You have to repent of all these things. Get delivered from them. Forgive and get free.

Profanity and gossip

Jesus said, "Not what goes into the mouth defiles a man; but what comes out of the mouth, this defiles a man" (Matt. 15:11, NKJV). What kind of words are you speaking? I believe people who use curse, gossip, backbite, and use profanity will have trouble maintaining the goodness in their land. These people are defiled, and their land is unclean.

When you engage in hateful speech, it is a sign that demons are in your life and manifesting through your mouth. Gossiping, backbiting, criticism, cursing, and profanity are signs of demonic occupation, and you must get them out.

The Blessing of Deliverance

Deliverance is such an important key to occupying the good land and sustaining a life within its borders. I encourage you to get copies of my books *Deliverance and Spiritual Warfare Manual*, *God's Covenant With You for Deliverance and Freedom*, and *Unshakeable*, which talks about double-mindedness, the manifestation of the spirits of rebellion and rejection—how they work together. These books will give you an understanding of the areas in which you may need deliverance. They will show you how to get prayer and deliverance that will command these spirits to come out of your life. They will even show you how to perform self-deliverance to maintain a place of strength and freedom.

You want to clear the land. You want the land to be blessed. You want to enjoy the glory and rain of heaven. You don't want anything in your land that defiles it. Deliverance puts you in a position for your land to be blessed and for prosperity, abundance, glory, joy, peace, and finances to flow in your life. All these things will come upon your land when it is cleared of the enemy's influence.

There is a blessing that comes with deliverance. Don't let anyone tell you otherwise. Deliverance is a ministry that will clear and cleanse your land so that you can receive the blessings of heaven. All those unclean demonic groups—those unclean demonic chains such as fear, lust, anger, hatred, bitterness, rejection, rebellion, and pride—will defile your land and move things into it that prevent the blessing of God. God blesses clean land—land that has been cleansed, redeemed, forgiven, and delivered. He pours His blessing, His rain from heaven, and His Spirit upon that land.

So get the land cleared. Clean out your land. Drive out anything in your land that is unclean, and let your faith rise for the good land, a land flowing with rivers and water, rain and abundance, and copper, silver, and bronze. It's a land of *chayil*, which means strength, power, wealth, wisdom, favor, and influence. In the good land you will lend to many and not borrow. You will be the head and not the tail. You will be blessed coming in and blessed going out. You will be blessed in the city and blessed in the field. In the good land God will take sickness and disease from your midst. That's living in the blessed land, the good land.

In this next section I want to take you through a scripture-by-scripture review of the attributes and characteristics of the good land. If you are familiar with my Topical Scripture Series, this section is much like that. I pray that you will be blessed as you read words directly from God's heart about the life and land He desires for you.

PART II

CHARACTERISTICS OF THE GOOD LAND AS REVEALED IN SCRIPTURE

Chapter 5

A LARGE AND WEALTHY PLACE

THE GOOD LAND is a large place. It is a place of more than enough room. There is room to grow and expand in the good land. You are not confined to small thinking, small believing, small prophetic flow, or small exploits! The good land has expansive provision, expansive anointing, expansive increase, and glory!

> He brought me forth also into a large place; he delivered me, because he delighted in me.
>
> —PSALM 18:19

> I called upon the LORD in distress: the LORD answered me, and set me in a large place.
>
> —PSALM 118:5

The Wisdom of God Brings You Into a Large Place

Wisdom is the best. Wisdom is better than fine gold. Wisdom will lead you in the paths of righteousness and judgment. You will inherit substance. Wisdom will fill your treasures.

> My fruit is better than gold, yea, than fine gold; and my revenue than choice silver. I lead in the way of righteousness, in the midst of the paths of judgment: that I may

69

cause those that love me to inherit substance; and I will fill their treasures.

—Proverbs 8:19–21

Wisdom, humility, and understanding are better than gold and silver. The best life is a life of wisdom. God wants to give you His wisdom. God wants you to have His best.

How much better it is to get wisdom than gold! And to get understanding is to be chosen above silver.

—Proverbs 16:16, amp

Wise people's houses are full of the best foods [or precious treasure] and olive oil, but fools waste [consume; swallow] everything they have.

—Proverbs 21:20, exb

Wisdom will fill your house with the best. Fools will not enjoy the best. God teaches us to profit. He teaches us what is best.

This is what the Lord, who saves you [your Redeemer], the Holy One of Israel, says: "I am the Lord your God, who teaches you to do what is good [what is best; or how to succeed], who leads you in the way you should go."

—Isaiah 48:17, exb

Submit Your Plans to the Lord and Receive God's Best

If you want God's best, you must submit your plans to Him. Many people don't do this, and they wonder why they don't enjoy God's best.

Commit thy works unto the Lord, and thy thoughts shall be established.

—Proverbs 16:3

Committing your works (submitting your plans) to the Lord is a key to being successful and having the best. Notice some different translations of this scripture:

> Commit your works to the LORD [submit and trust them to Him], and your plans will succeed [if you respond to His will and guidance].
>
> —PROVERBS 16:3, AMP

> Put GOD in charge of your work, then what you've planned will take place.
>
> —PROVERBS 16:3, MSG

> Before you do anything, put your trust totally in God and not in yourself. Then every plan you make will succeed.
>
> —PROVERBS 16:3, TPT

> Show thy works to the Lord; and thy thoughts shall be (ad)dressed. (Commit thy plans to the Lord; and they shall succeed.)
>
> —PROVERBS 16:3, WYC

Trust in the Lord and Receive God's Best

As you see the translations of Proverbs 16:3 above, notice how being able to commit your plans to God has a lot to do with being able to trust Him. Therefore, trusting in the Lord is another key to receiving God's best. You cannot lean on your own understanding. God will direct your path when you acknowledge Him in all your ways.

> Trust in the LORD with all thine heart; and lean not unto thine own understanding. In all thy ways acknowledge him, and he shall direct thy paths.
>
> —PROVERBS 3:5–6

God's plans for your life are the best. God's thoughts for you are the best.

> For I know the thoughts that I think toward you, saith the LORD, thoughts of peace, and not of evil, to give you an expected end.
>
> —JEREMIAH 29:11

This is the heart of God for His people. God does not take pleasure when you are not enlarged and don't receive His best plan for your life. God's plans are plans of peace (shalom) and prosperity, and He takes pleasure in the prosperity of His servants.

> To those who want the best for me, I wish them joy and happiness. May they always say, "Praise the LORD, who wants what is best for his servant."
>
> —JEREMIAH 29:11, ERV

In other words, God is pleased when we have the best.

God Desires for You to Have the Best Successes, Victories, and Blessings

You can have the best advice and strategies. This will give you the best success.

> If you solicit good advice, then your plans will succeed. So don't charge into battle without wisdom, for wars are won by skillful strategy.
>
> —PROVERBS 20:18, TPT

You will win your battles because of wisdom and strategy. Wisdom will give you the best victories.

> Wise strategy is necessary to wage war, and with many astute advisers you'll see the path to victory more clearly.
>
> —PROVERBS 24:6, TPT

Jesus came that we might have abundant life (John 10:10). The abundant life is the best life. Life in the Spirit is the best life. A life of wisdom is the best life. Don't settle for a life that is not the best. The best life is a life of prosperity and abundance. Just as God gave David the best blessings, you can believe God for His best and choicest blessings.

> For You met him with the best blessings. You set on his head a crown of pure gold.
>
> —Psalm 21:4, tlv

The Best Satisfies You

We should not waste our time or money on anything less than the best. The best gives you satisfaction.

> Why do you spend money on what cannot nourish you and your wages on what does not satisfy you? Listen carefully to me: Eat what is good, and enjoy the best foods.
>
> —Isaiah 55:2, gw

> They ate cheese from cows and drank milk from sheep and goats. He gave them fat from lambs, rams from the stock of Bashan, male goats, and the best wheat. They drank the blood-red wine of grapes.
>
> —Deuteronomy 32:14, gw

Fatness: a Picture of Wealth, Increase, and Plenty

Fat is a picture of richness. The Israelites were to eat the fat of the land in Egypt.

> And take your father and your households, and come unto me: and I will give you the good of the land of Egypt, and ye shall eat the fat of the land.
>
> —Genesis 45:18

According to the writers at The Simple Answers:

> Fat is considered by many cultures, particularly those in
> the middle east, to be a delicacy. And as we saw, only
> the visceral fat is prohibited. Here God promises that
> they will eat the fat of the land. There is also a dual
> meaning because here the fat (the same Hebrew word is
> used as elsewhere in Leviticus) is pictured as a blessing of
> plenty of food and good land. Because the fat is one of
> the end products of metabolism in the body, God uses it
> to represent the end product of working a good produc-
> tive land—in that sense, the fat would also represent the
> bottles of wine and oil, the barns full of hay and the bins
> full of grain for the next year.[1]

Fat in your body is excess. Your body stores fat. Fat is therefore a picture of increase. While this is true and serves the
purpose for showing the spiritual revelation, please be mindful
that in the United States and other Westernized cultures, physical fatness—what we may call *obesity* in our natural and physical bodies—is harmful, and it is occurring in epidemic rates
in our country. Many are dying because of various spiritual,
emotional, and physical issues that lead to imbalance, as well
as issues of self-control that lead to overeating and in some
cases deadly diseases such as heart disease and diabetes.

I talk about the spiritual roots of many diseases we call
"lifestyle diseases" in my book *Unshakeable*. Temperance, mod-
eration, and self-control are necessary when it comes to our
physical bodies, but in the spirit realm God loves to lavish us
with abundance and excess as we come into the kingdom and
the good land. He is a good heavenly Father, the King of the
invisible kingdom, who loves to bestow lavish gifts upon His
sons and daughters.

The writers at The Simple Answer continue:

So here is the conclusion: as God blesses a righteous person or nation, they accumulate excess; called in the Bible "increase." As a healthy body grows on good food, it accumulates a healthy excess which it stores back called "fat."[2]

Fat is also a picture of "the best." As I mentioned earlier, the word *best* in Hebrew is *heleb* or *cheleb* and means "fat…the richest or choice part: best…finest, grease, marrow…abundance (of products of the land)."[3]

You grow fat when you partake of "the best." You grow fat when you partake of the richness of God's Word. You grow fat when you are in the richness of God's presence and glory. Yokes are destroyed in your life. Your neck becomes too large for the enemy's yokes.

Fatness, pride, and rebellion

There is also a negative side to fatness. The Israelites got fat and rebelled. Fatness and prosperity can lead to pride and rebellion.

But Jeshurun waxed fat, and kicked: thou art waxen fat, thou art grown thick, thou art covered with fatness; then he forsook God which made him, and lightly esteemed the Rock of his salvation.

—Deuteronomy 32:15

The Easy-to-Read Version says it this way:

But Jeshurun became fat and kicked like a bull. (Yes, you people were fed well and became full and fat.) They left the God who made them! They ran away from the Rock who saved them.

—Deuteronomy 32:15, erv

We must be careful when we become blessed and free. We must be careful not to become prideful. Humility is always the key to maintaining freedom and walking in the blessings of God.

Chaim Bentorah says, "I am told by a farmer that a well fed cow will grow insolent and rebellious and will end up kicking you if you are not careful. The cow becomes spoiled and demanding. That appears to be the idea behind this verse [Deut. 32:15]. We can grow fat and lazy with God's blessings and then when he removes one, we begin to whine and kick."[4]

God warned the Israelites about becoming full and forgetting Him. The proud are enclosed in their own fat (Ps. 17:10). Your heart can become gross (fat, thick). (See Matthew 13:15.)

> When thou hast eaten and art full, then thou shalt bless the LORD thy God for the good land which he hath given thee. Beware that thou forget not the LORD thy God, in not keeping his commandments, and his judgments, and his statutes, which I command thee this day: lest when thou hast eaten and art full, and hast built goodly houses, and dwelt therein; and when thy herds and thy flocks multiply, and thy silver and thy gold is multiplied, and all that thou hast is multiplied; then thine heart be lifted up, and thou forget the LORD thy God, which brought thee forth out of the land of Egypt, from the house of bondage.
>
> —DEUTERONOMY 8:10–14

In other words, don't allow yourself to become lifted up. Don't forget the One who bursts your bonds and increases you. Don't forget the One who anoints you to prosper and get wealth (Deut. 8:18) Humility and meekness should be the standard for your life. Humility brings riches and honor (Prov. 22:4). Humility brings promotion. Never become fat and proud.

Fatness and the spirit of Eglon

The wicked like to get fat off what belongs to the people of God. I call this the spirit of Eglon. Eglon and the Moabites oppressed Israel.

> And he brought the present unto Eglon king of Moab: and Eglon was a very fat man.
>
> —Judges 3:17

God sent Ehud to kill Eglon and free Israel from his control. Ehud stuck a dagger into Eglon, and the dagger was enclosed in the fat. Eglon could not withdraw the dagger, and he died.

Fatness and the wicked

Here is an interesting verse from the Book of Job concerning the wicked swallowing riches:

> He hath swallowed down riches, and he shall vomit them up again: God shall cast them out of his belly.
>
> —Job 20:15

This is a picture of God's judgment against wickedness, pride, and rebellion. "Their eyes stand out with fatness: they have more than heart could wish" (Ps. 73:7). God casts His wrath upon them.

> When he is about to fill his belly, God shall cast the fury of his wrath upon him, and shall rain it upon him while he is eating.
>
> —Job 20:23

God judged the wicked who got fat off destroying His people.

> Because ye were glad, because ye rejoiced, O ye destroyers of mine heritage, because ye are grown fat as the heifer at grass, and bellow as bulls.
>
> —Jeremiah 50:11

God judged the rich who got fat by oppressing the poor. They were like fat cows engorging themselves. In other words, you should not get fat by using people.

> You have lived luxuriously on the land [the fat of the land] and have indulged yourselves. You have fattened your hearts for the day of slaughter.
>
> —JAMES 5:5, HCSB

Amos called the women of Samaria "fat cows." They were oppressing the poor and robbing the needy.

> Listen to this message, you fat cows from Bashan, who live on the Samaritan mountains, who oppress the poor, who rob the needy, and who constantly ask your husbands for one more drink!
>
> —AMOS 4:1, ISV

We are delivered from sin and bondage to move into the good land. We are delivered to go to a large place, a wealthy place. The good land is a large place. It is a place of more than enough room. There is room to grow and expand in the good land.

Chapter 6

A LAND OF MILK AND HONEY

THE GOOD LAND is a land of milk and honey. Milk and honey represent sweetness, love, intimacy, nourishment, and abundance. Milk particularly is a picture of consolation and comfort. It also represents the Word of God and purity. Honey is a picture of the sweetness of the prophetic word. Honey represents pleasant words that bring healing and restoration.

God brought the Israelites into a land full of milk and honey. Jonathan Cohen, the writer of "Why Milk and Honey," states the following:

> For us, "milk and honey" originates in the Hebrew Bible in God's description of the country lying between the Mediterranean Sea and the Jordan River, namely, Canaan. It is first described as "a good and spacious land, a land flowing with milk and honey..."
>
> We generally accept the received definition of "milk and honey" as a metaphor meaning all good things—God's blessings; and that the Promised Land must have been a land of extraordinary fertility. The phrase "flowing with milk and honey" is understood to be hyperbolically descriptive of the land's richness; hence, its current use to express the abundance of pure means of enjoyment.
>
> The original Hebrew (transliterated) is "e-retz za-vat

ha-lav oo–d'vash"; literally, *land* (e-retz) *flowing with* (za-vat) *milk* (ha-lav) *and* (oo–) *honey* (d'vash). The word translated as "flowing" comes from the verb "zoov" which means to flow or gush. Key to understanding this word in the biblical context is an appreciation of its human sexual associations, given that variants of it are used elsewhere in the Bible to denote the bodily fluids issued from the genitals of either a woman or a man.

Thus, in the Hebrew, the word "za-vat" suggests the idea of the land's gushing milk and honey in a sudden and copious flow, as well as its oozing them, and dripping them.[1]

> Thou shalt also suck the milk of the Gentiles, and shalt suck the breast of kings: and thou shalt know that I the Lord am thy Saviour and thy Redeemer, the mighty One of Jacob.
>
> —Isaiah 60:16

As I mentioned above, milk is a picture of consolation and comfort; it comes with the glory. The good land is a place of glory.

> That ye may suck, and be satisfied with the breasts of her consolations; that ye may milk out, and be delighted with the abundance of her glory.
>
> —Isaiah 66:11

Milk represents the Word. The Word of God provides strength. The Word of God establishes and refreshes you. The Word of God strengthens you. The Word of God changes your mind-set.

> As newborn babes, desire the sincere milk of the word, that ye may grow thereby.
>
> —1 Peter 2:2

Milk also represents purity. The good land is a place of purity.

> Her Nazarites were purer than snow, they were whiter
> than milk, they were more ruddy in body than rubies,
> their polishing was of sapphire.
>
> —LAMENTATIONS 4:7

Honey and Sweetness

Honey represents sweetness. Honey is a picture of the sweetness of the prophetic word. One dimension of the prophetic anointing is movement. Prophetic people are constantly moving and advancing. Prophetic ministries are on the go in the realm of the spirit. They are not stagnant and dry. They carry a fresh word, a fresh anointing, and fresh vision.

When you receive a prophetic word, it is sweet! It blesses you, encourages you, and enlightens you. The prophetic will lead you into the good land. As God speaks, His instructions become clear.

> And he said unto me, Son of man, cause thy belly to eat,
> and fill thy bowels with this roll that I give thee. Then did
> I eat it; and it was in my mouth as honey for sweetness.
>
> —EZEKIEL 3:3

> More to be desired are they than gold, yea, than much
> fine gold: sweeter also than honey and the honeycomb.
>
> —PSALM 19:10

Honey, Wheat, and Oil

Honey from the rock satisfies. The good land is full of honey and is also full of wheat. Wheat represents harvest and is the main ingredient of bread. Jesus is the Bread of Life. Bread satisfies and strengthens the heart.

> He should have fed them also with the finest of the
> wheat: and with honey out of the rock should I have
> satisfied thee.
>
> —Psalm 81:16

Honey and oil come from the rock. Jesus is the rock.

> He made him ride on the high places of the earth, that he
> might eat the increase of the fields; and he made him to
> suck honey out of the rock, and oil out of the flinty rock.
>
> —Deuteronomy 32:13

Honey Is Healing and Restorative

Honey represents pleasant words that bring healing and restoration. Words from the Lord will heal your heart, your ministry, and your body. In fact one of the greatest healing methods is to simply read and confess healing scriptures. The Word of God contains healing power for every facet of your life.

> Pleasant words are as an honeycomb, sweet to the soul,
> and health to the bones.
>
> —Proverbs 16:24

We eat honey because it is good. Honey is sweet to the taste.

> My son, eat thou honey, because it is good; and the honeycomb, which is sweet to thy taste.
>
> —Proverbs 24:13

> O taste and see that the Lord is good: blessed is the
> man that trusteth in him.
>
> —Psalm 34:8

Milk and Honey Represent
Intimacy and Love

Honey and milk represent intimacy and love. The good land is a place of intimacy with the Father. It is a place of love relationships, worship, prayer, and seeking. The good land is a place of communion with God.

> Thy lips, O my spouse, drop as the honeycomb: honey and milk are under thy tongue; and the smell of thy garments is like the smell of Lebanon.
>
> —Song of Solomon 4:11

> I am come into my garden, my sister, my spouse: I have gathered my myrrh with my spice; I have eaten my honeycomb with my honey; I have drunk my wine with my milk: eat, O friends; drink, yea, drink abundantly, O beloved.
>
> —Song of Solomon 5:1

Milk and Beauty

Milk is also a picture of beauty. God wants to reveal His beauty to you. He wants to show you how beautiful His plans are, how beautiful His kingdom is, and how beautiful His Word is. God wants to release beauty into your life. He wants to do things for you that release beauty. He wants to bring you into greater blessings.

> His eyes are as the eyes of doves by the rivers of waters, washed with milk, and fitly set.
>
> —Song of Solomon 5:12

Milk, Wine, Blessing, and Prosperity

Milk and wine are pictures of blessing and prosperity. You cannot think about the good land without thinking about blessings and prosperity.

> His eyes shall be red with wine, and his teeth white with milk.
>
> —Genesis 49:12

Vines produce wine, and wine is another picture of the Holy Spirit. God promised good wine. New wine, milk, and water are pictures of kingdom living. Kingdom living is prosperous living.

> And it shall come to pass in that day, that the mountains shall drop down new wine, and the hills shall flow with milk, and all the rivers of Judah shall flow with waters, and a fountain shall come forth out of the house of the LORD, and shall water the valley of Shittim.
>
> —JOEL 3:18

The mountains drop sweet wine and the hills flow with milk in the good land.

> Behold, the days come, saith the LORD, that the plowman shall overtake the reaper, and the treader of grapes him that soweth seed; and the mountains shall drop sweet wine, and all the hills shall melt.
>
> —AMOS 9:13

Honey and Butter

The good land has honey and butter. Butter comes from the abundance of milk.

> And it shall come to pass, for the abundance of milk that they shall give he shall eat butter: for butter and honey shall every one eat that is left in the land.
>
> —ISAIAH 7:22

He shall not see the rivers, the floods, the brooks of honey and butter.

> —JOB 20:17

> Butter of kine, and milk of sheep, with fat of lambs, and rams of the breed of Bashan, and goats, with the fat of

> kidneys of wheat; and thou didst drink the pure blood
> of the grape.
>
> —Deuteronomy 32:14

Butter is richness and another picture of abundance and prosperity.

> When I washed my steps with butter, and the rock
> poured me out rivers of oil.
>
> —Job 29:6

Butter and honey are pictures of the critical gifts of discernment and wisdom. These two gifts can save your life! The wisdom of God will protect you, guide you, and establish you. Discernment will reveal errors and flaws, causing you to avoid calamity.

> Butter and honey shall he eat, that he may know to
> refuse the evil, and choose the good.
>
> —Isaiah 7:15

Bees

The good land is a land of bees. Bees live in gardens, they produce honey, and they pollinate. Plants and flowers grow because of pollination. The good land is a green land. It is the garden of the Lord. It is a land of green trees. Green also represents prosperity and abundance.

Jane Birch states the following:

> The phrase "milk and honey" is an idiom. According to
> the Oxford English Dictionary, it means "prosperity and
> abundance; richness of produce; plenty, comfort; also
> attrib." Milk and honey (like corn and wine) are sym-
> bols of fertility that appear in the most ancient writings.
> Bees are critical to plant production. Even today, about
> a third of the human food supply depends on insect

pollination, and bees are the main pollinators. A land that flows with honey is a land where bees are doing their work, enabling plants [to] grow, so the milk can flow from animals to feed their young. When the spies sent by Moses to scout out the Promised Land wanted to show evidence that the land was flowing with milk and honey, they brought back grapes, pomegranates, and figs (Numbers 13:23–27).[2]

Bees cause the land to bud and blossom. The good land is likened unto Eden, the garden of the Lord.

For the LORD shall comfort Zion: he will comfort all her waste places; and he will make her wilderness like Eden, and her desert like the garden of the LORD; joy and gladness shall be found therein, thanksgiving, and the voice of melody.

—ISAIAH 51:3

And they spake unto all the company of the children of Israel, saying, The land, which we passed through to search it, is an exceeding good land.

—NUMBERS 14:7

The land is not only good, but "exceeding good."

God wants to bring you into a land flowing with milk and honey where you will experience a flow of sweet abundance, enlargement, and prosperity.

Chapter 7

A LAND OF WATER, PLENTY, SATISFACTION, FLOURISHING, AND ABUNDANCE

THE GOOD LAND is a land of water, rain, fountains, springs, satisfaction, and plenty. Water represents refreshing and blessing. Water represents the Holy Spirit. The good land is a land that brings satisfaction. You can eat and be full. The good land is a land of plenty. There is no lack in the good land. In Him we have a well of water springing up into everlasting life. And in the good land we need to be refreshed in our assignments, callings, and lives.

Springs of Water

They shall not hunger nor thirst; neither shall the heat nor sun smite them: for he that hath mercy on them shall lead them, even by the springs of water shall he guide them.

—ISAIAH 49:10

Caleb gave his daughter springs in the good land.

And it came to pass, as she came unto him, that she moved him to ask of her father a field: and she lighted off her ass; and Caleb said unto her, What wouldest thou?

> Who answered, Give me a blessing; for thou hast
> given me a south land; give me also springs of water. And
> he gave her the upper springs, and the nether springs.
>
> —JOSHUA 15:18–19

We have a well of water springing up into everlasting life.
We never have to be dry and dusty! We have the rivers of living
water inside of us. We are not only refreshed but also carry
refreshing that can greatly bless others. Christians should live
out of the inner rivers.

> But whosoever drinketh of the water that I shall give
> him shall never thirst; but the water that I shall give
> him shall be in him a well of water springing up into
> everlasting life.
>
> —JOHN 4:14

Springs of living water flow from our innermost being.

> He that believeth on me, as the scripture hath said, out
> of his belly shall flow rivers of living water.
>
> —JOHN 7:38

> For the LORD thy God bringeth thee into a good land,
> a land of brooks of water, of fountains and depths that
> spring out of valleys and hills.
>
> —DEUTERONOMY 8:7

The River of God

The river of God, a river of life, flows in the good land.

> Thou visitest the earth, and waterest it: thou greatly
> enrichest it with the river of God, which is full of water:
> thou preparest them corn, when thou hast so provided
> for it.
>
> —PSALM 65:9

> The pastures are clothed with flocks; the valleys also are
> covered over with corn; they shout for joy, they also sing.
> —Psalm 65:13

The Dew of Mount Hermon

The good land has a goodly mountain called Mount Hermon,
which is another picture of blessing and prosperity.

> I pray, let me go over and see the good land that is beyond
> the Jordan, that good hill country [with Hermon] and
> Lebanon.
> —Deuteronomy 3:25, amp

Mount Hermon is a place of dew. Dew is moisture. The
good land is a moist land.

> As the dew of Hermon, and as the dew that descended
> upon the mountains of Zion: for there the Lord com-
> manded the blessing, even life for evermore.
> —Psalm 133:3

Abundance of Rain

The good land receives an abundance of rain. Rain falls from
heaven in both the natural and spiritual realms as a sign of
blessing. The Lord can come to us like the rain. The rain—
showers of blessing, increase, and water for our seed—increases
us and makes us lenders and not borrowers. The rain of heaven
waters the seed and brings life to the areas of our lives that are
still germinating.

> That I will give you the rain of your land in his due
> season, the first rain and the latter rain, that thou mayest
> gather in thy corn, and thy wine, and thine oil.
> —Deuteronomy 11:14

The rain causes us to gather corn, wine, and oil—our harvest. The Lord comes to us as the rain.

> Then shall we know, if we follow on to know the LORD: his going forth is prepared as the morning; and he shall come unto us as the rain, as the latter and former rain unto the earth.
>
> —Hosea 6:3

The Lord falls upon us as the rain in the good land. The rain brings revival and refreshing.

> He shall come down like rain upon the mown grass: as showers that water the earth.
>
> —Psalm 72:6

The Lord gives a plentiful rain in the good land. We are confirmed and strengthened by this rain. Rain also represents the favor of the King. The good land is a land of favor.

> Thou, O God, didst send a plentiful rain, whereby thou didst confirm thine inheritance, when it was weary.
>
> —Psalm 68:9

> In the light of the king's countenance is life; and his favour is as a cloud of the latter rain.
>
> —Proverbs 16:15

> When thou hast eaten and art full, then thou shalt bless the LORD thy God for the good land which he hath given thee.
>
> —Deuteronomy 8:10

Satisfaction and Plenty

The good land is a land that brings satisfaction; you can eat and be full. The good land is also a land of plenty; there is no lack in the good land.

> A land of wheat and barley, of vines and fig trees and
> pomegranates, a land of olive oil and honey.
>
> —DEUTERONOMY 8:8, NKJV

There is fatness that satisfies us in the house of the Lord. We
should receive the best in the house of the Lord.

> They shall be abundantly satisfied with the fatness of thy
> house; and thou shalt make them drink of the river of
> thy pleasures.
>
> —PSALM 36:8

We experience the joy of the Lord when we eat the fat.

> Then he said unto them, Go your way, eat the fat, and
> drink the sweet, and send portions unto them for whom
> nothing is prepared: for this day is holy unto our LORD:
> neither be ye sorry; for the joy of the LORD is your
> strength.
>
> —NEHEMIAH 8:10

The blessing brings fatness (which essentially means the
best). God will bless you with the best in the good land.

> And Isaac his father answered and said unto him, Behold,
> thy dwelling shall be the fatness of the earth, and of the
> dew of heaven from above.
>
> —GENESIS 27:39

The good land is a land of corn and wine. We have plenty of
corn, wine, and oil in the good land. We are satisfied.

> Therefore God give thee of the dew of heaven, and the
> fatness of the earth, and plenty of corn and wine.
>
> —GENESIS 27:28

> Yea, the LORD will answer and say unto his people,
> Behold, I will send you corn, and wine, and oil, and ye

shall be satisfied therewith: and I will no more make you
a reproach among the heathen.

—JOEL 2:19

Fat and Flourishing

They shall still bring forth fruit in old age; they shall be
fat and flourishing.

—PSALM 92:14

In Psalm 92:12–14 the righteous are described as being "planted
in the house of the LORD" and are said to "grow like a cedar"
and "flourish like the palm tree." They will continue bearing
fruit even in their old age. They shall be "fat and flourishing."
The phrase *fat and flourishing* is found in the King James
Version of the Bible but is translated using a variety of words
in different English versions, including "full of sap and green"
(ESV), "healthy and green" (HCSB), "luxuriant and green" (ISV),
"fat and luxuriant" (LEB), "filled with vitality and have many
leaves" (NET), "fresh and green" (NIV), and "fresh and flourishing" (NKJV).

In Isaiah 25, Isaiah's prophecy shows that fatness is a picture of the kingdom. In verse 6 he says, "And in this mountain shall the LORD of hosts make unto all people a feast of fat
things, a feast of wines on the lees, of fat things full of marrow,
of wines on the lees well refined." Here we find that fatness
is a picture of abundance, anointing, richness, growth, and
increase. In other words, you can burst forth into abundance
through fatness.

Fatness is a picture of satisfaction. God satisfies us with fatness. There are many verses in the Bible that speak of fat as a
picture of growth and prosperity. Here are some of them:

They shall be abundantly satisfied with the fatness of thy house; and thou shalt make them drink of the river of thy pleasures.

—PSALM 36:8

My soul shall be satisfied as with marrow and fatness; and my mouth shall praise thee with joyful lips.

—PSALM 63:5

Thou crownest the year with thy goodness; and thy paths drop fatness.

—PSALM 65:11

And I will satiate the soul of the priests with fatness, and my people shall be satisfied with my goodness, saith the LORD.

—JEREMIAH 31:14

Fruitfulness and Abundance

Sweetness and love

The good land is a land of pomegranates and figs. Pomegranates represent fruitfulness, sweetness, abundance, beauty, and love.

And they came unto the brook of Eshcol, and cut down from thence a branch with one cluster of grapes, and they bare it between two upon a staff; and they brought of the pomegranates, and of the figs.

—NUMBERS 13:23

Thy plants are an orchard of pomegranates, with pleasant fruits; camphire, with spikenard.

—SONG OF SOLOMON 4:13

I went down into the garden of nuts to see the fruits of the valley, and to see whether the vine flourished and the pomegranates budded.

—SONG OF SOLOMON 6:11

> Let us get up early to the vineyards; let us see if the vine
> flourish, whether the tender grape appear, and the pome-
> granates bud forth: there will I give thee my loves.
>
> —SONG OF SOLOMON 7:12

The good land is a land of fig trees. Figs are another symbol
of sweetness and love. The fig tree also represents fruitfulness
and abundance. Jesus cursed the fig tree because it had leaves
but no fruit. (See Mark 11:12–25.)

> The fig tree putteth forth her green figs, and the vines
> with the tender grape give a good smell. Arise, my love,
> my fair one, and come away.
>
> —SONG OF SOLOMON 2:13

Prosperity and the best

Remember the word *best* means "fatness" or "grease." There
are several verses that mention fatness. Fatness is a picture of
prosperity and the best. Your soul can be satisfied with marrow
and fatness.

> My soul shall be satisfied as with marrow and fatness;
> and my mouth shall praise thee with joyful lips.
>
> —PSALM 63:5

There is fatness and marrow (the best) in the kingdom (the
mountain of the Lord).

> And in this mountain shall the LORD of hosts make
> unto all people a feast of fat things, a feast of wines on
> the lees, of fat things full of marrow, of wines on the
> lees well refined.
>
> —ISAIAH 25:6

We can enjoy a feast of the finest in the kingdom.

> They shall still bring forth fruit in old age; they shall be
> fat and flourishing.
>
> —Psalm 92:14

The land of Canaan produced the best crops and produce.

> May the Lord bless their land with crops, the best gift
> the sun can give, the best produce of each month.
>
> —Deuteronomy 33:14, GW

The hills yielded the best.

> The finest fruits from the oldest mountains, the best
> from the ancient hills.
>
> —Deuteronomy 33:15, GW

> All the best of the fresh [olive] oil, and all the best of the
> new wine and of the grain, the first fruits of those which
> they give to the Lord, I give them to you.
>
> —Numbers 18:12, AMP

We are priests and kings in the good land. Our souls are
satiated with fatness.

> And I will satiate the soul of the priests with fatness, and
> my people shall be satisfied with my goodness, saith the
> Lord.
>
> —Jeremiah 31:14

Chapter 8

A LAND WHERE THE
ANOINTING FLOWS LIKE OIL

THE GOOD LAND is a land rich in oil from the olive. Olive oil represents fatness and the anointing. The anointing is powerful and precious. When the anointing is present and working, you can do things you could not normally do. With the anointing of the Holy Spirit—which is often represented in Scripture by oil, which is 100 percent fat—you are empowered and strengthened.

> Thou shalt have olive trees throughout all thy coasts, but thou shalt not anoint thyself with the oil; for thine olive shall cast his fruit.
>
> —DEUTERONOMY 28:40

> And houses full of all good things, which thou filledst not, and wells digged, which thou diggedst not, vineyards and olive trees, which thou plantedst not; when thou shalt have eaten and be full.
>
> —DEUTERONOMY 6:11

Yokes are broken because of the fat (anointing). You cannot enjoy the best when you are in bondage. The anointing breaks yokes and takes you from the worst to the best. We need anointed preaching, teaching, and worship to help us know how to cross over into the good land.

> So it will be in that day, that the burden of the Assyrian will be removed from your shoulders and his yoke from your neck. The yoke will be broken because of the fat.
> —ISAIAH 10:27, AMP

Other translations of this verse say, "because your neck will be too large," (NET) and "because you have grown fat" (GW). In other words, you grow and burst out of your bonds. Remember, *best* in Hebrew means "fat" or "greasy." To anoint means "to smear with oil or make greasy." The anointing, as we know, also represents the power of the Holy Spirit. The anointing of God will open the way for you to walk in and have the best. The anointing will cause you to grow fat and burst free from your bonds. The Young's Literal Translation says, "and destroyed hath been the yoke, because of prosperity."

Burst Free!

> For it shall come to pass in that day, saith the LORD of hosts, that I will break his yoke from off thy neck, and will burst thy bonds, and strangers shall no more serve themselves of him.
> —JEREMIAH 30:8

Burst your bonds and experience the best. Burst out of failure and frustration. Don't let people and bad doctrine keep you mediocre and average. Break out into the best.

In looking at Isaiah 10:27 again, the Amplified version says the Assyrian yoke of bondage around Israel's neck would be broken "because of the fat." This came as a shock to me when I read this translation. All my life as a Pentecostal I heard that the yoke was destroyed because of the anointing. I had never heard anyone preach that it was "because of the fat." What does this mean?

I began to look up other translations of this verse, and I was amazed. Here are some of the translations I found:

> And it shall be in that day that the burden of [the Assyrian] shall depart from your shoulders, and his yoke from your neck. The yoke shall be destroyed *because of fatness* [which prevents it from going around your neck].
> —ISAIAH 10:27, AMPC, EMPHASIS ADDED

> On that day his burden will fall from your shoulders, and his yoke from your neck. The yoke will be broken *because your neck will be too large.*
> —ISAIAH 10:27, CSB, EMPHASIS ADDED

> On that day his burden will fall from your shoulders and his yoke from your neck; the yoke will be *destroyed by your prosperity.*
> —ISAIAH 10:27, CJB, EMPHASIS ADDED

> At that time their burden will be removed from your shoulders. Their yoke will be removed from your neck. The yoke will be torn away *because you have grown fat.*
> —ISAIAH 10:27, GW, EMPHASIS ADDED

> At that time their burden will be removed from your shoulders. Their yoke will be removed from your neck. The yoke will be torn away *because you have grown fat.*
> —ISAIAH 10:27, NOG, EMPHASIS ADDED

> People of Zion, in days to come he will help you. He will lift the heavy load of the Assyrians from your shoulders. He will remove their yokes from your necks. Their yokes will be broken *because you have become so strong.*
> —ISAIAH 10:27, NIRV, EMPHASIS ADDED

I then found an article by author and radio show host Dr. Michael L. Brown, in which he states the following:

> The New International Version expresses it well: "In that day their burden will be lifted from your shoulders, their yoke from your neck; the yoke will be broken because you have grown so fat."
>
> Do you get the picture? Here is an ox with a yoke on its neck, enslaving it to the will of its master, forcing it to a life of servitude. But eventually, it gets so healthy and fat that the yoke simply bursts from off its neck. That ox is now free![1]

This is the freedom that Christ bought for us. Yokes represent bondage and slavery. They prevent us from moving free and put us in servitude to a master like oxen yoked to plow the fields. The yoke was placed around the necks of the oxen. It made them work hard. Jesus' yoke is easy (Matt. 11:30). The yoke of the enemy is hard. Israel had come under the yoke of the Assyrians, and Isaiah prophesied their deliverance.

> As a consequence of Israel's rejection of God, Isaiah prophesied that the Lord would raise up the Assyrians to oppress them. Yet, God, in His mercy, revealed that the day would come when the faithful remnant would break free from the Assyrians. Isaiah declared that the yoke of oppression would be broken off of their neck by the Anointing. The English translation of this verse uses the phrase, "Anointing oil." It is from this idea that the phrase—"the Anointing breaks the yoke"—is derived. However, Isaiah did not use the Hebrew word for Anointing, "Mashach." He used the word, "Shamen," which means, "fatness." In essence, Isaiah was stating that their freedom from the yoke of oppression would come as they grew fat. The metaphor is that of a young ox who has a yoke placed around his neck. As he grows

fat and healthy he expands. As the ox continues to expand he breaks out of the yoke that will no longer fit around his neck."[2]

In other words, you can become so fat that no yoke can be put on your shoulder. You can outgrow bondage. The anointing will bring prosperity, and prosperity will destroy the yoke.

Building upon his point in the quote just above, Brad Sullivan goes on to say that "this insight provides an understanding into how the anointing breaks the yoke. The Anointing of the Holy Spirit causes us to grow fat and to increase. As expansion comes, it causes us to break out of the yoke that once held us."[3]

Pastor Harold Miller Jr. says this:

Now when I looked at this text in some of the English versions other than the KJV/NKJV (King James Version/ New King James Version), I discovered that where the KJV/NKJV use the term "anointing," most of the other English versions use the term "fat" or some derivative of it such as "fatness." When I looked at the text in the Hebrew and conducted some lexical research, I also discovered that the word the KJV/NKJV translates as "anointing" is the Hebrew word: "shemen" or "semen." According [to] the TWOT (Theological Wordbook of the Old Testament) the primary meaning of this Hebrew word is "fat" and "oil." It is used to covey the idea of prosperity and well-being. The idea in Isaiah 10:27 is that the Assyrian yoke would be broken or destroyed because like oxen that have grown fat, the yoke would be broken and destroyed by Israel's neck becoming too large to be contained by it! It [is] also interesting to note that, of all the occurrences of this word in the Hebrew text (nearly 200 times!), this is the only occurrence where the KJV/ NKJV translates it as "anointing." All the other times, it is translated as fat, fatness, richness, or fertile. And even

where the idea of anointing is clearly present, shemen
or semen is translated as "oil" and is always found com-
bined with the Hebrew word "mashach," which means
to smear or anoint."[4]

Here is an interesting point about oxen from Dr. Michelle
Corral:

In Biblical times, when a farmer would purchase a
yoke of oxen, if he chose oxen with thin necks it meant
those oxen turned and resisted the pull of the plow. If
he chose oxen with fat flabby necks it meant the oxen
never resisted but turned every way the plow was led.
Eventually the neck of the oxen that never resisted
became so fat with the fats (like oil) in the neck that the
yoke would burst.[5]

God will burst your bonds. He will cause you to grow and
break free.

For now will I break his yoke from off thee, and will
burst thy bonds in sunder.

—NAHUM 1:13

To *burst* means to "break open or apart suddenly and vio-
lently, especially as a result of an impact or internal pressure."[6]

You begin to experience God's best when you grow fat and
healthy spiritually. You cannot be spiritually unhealthy and
expect to have the best. You can outgrow the worst of your
past. You can outgrow your limitations and failures.

Chapter 9

A LAND OVERFLOWING WITH GOODNESS, GROWTH, AND EXCELLENCE

THE GOOD LAND is a land of God's abundant goodness. There is goodness and mercy in the good land. The good land is the place in which we can believe God for His goodness. It is the land of the living. We will look at scriptures that show us how God's goodness is connected to fatness, which as we have discovered is another picture of prosperity and abundance. In the good land we are satisfied with God's goodness. We grow and flourish in the excellence of the good land.

The good land is a land of God's abundant goodness and mercy.

> And the LORD passed by before him, and proclaimed, The LORD, the LORD God, merciful and gracious, long-suffering, and abundant in goodness and truth.
>
> —EXODUS 34:6

> Surely goodness and mercy shall follow me all the days of my life: and I will dwell in the house of the LORD for ever.
>
> —PSALM 23:6

We can believe for God's goodness in the good land. His goodness is great.

> I had fainted, unless I had believed to see the goodness of the Lord in the land of the living.
>
> —Psalm 27:13

> Oh how great is thy goodness, which thou hast laid up for them that fear thee; which thou hast wrought for them that trust in thee before the sons of men!
>
> —Psalm 31:19

> He loveth righteousness and judgment: the earth is full of the goodness of the Lord.
>
> —Psalm 33:5

> Blessed is the man whom thou choosest, and causest to approach unto thee, that he may dwell in thy courts: we shall be satisfied with the goodness of thy house, even of thy holy temple.
>
> —Psalm 65:4

The good land is a land of praise. We praise the Lord for His goodness and wonderful works.

> Oh that men would praise the Lord for his goodness, and for his wonderful works to the children of men!
>
> —Psalm 107:8

> My goodness, and my fortress; my high tower, and my deliverer; my shield, and he in whom I trust; who subdueth my people under me.
>
> —Psalm 144:2

> They shall abundantly utter the memory of thy great goodness, and shall sing of thy righteousness.
>
> —Psalm 145:7

Goodness is prosperity. As we have already discovered, the good land is a land of prosperity.

> And it shall be to me a name of joy, a praise and an honour before all the nations of the earth, which shall hear all the good that I do unto them: and they shall fear and tremble for all the goodness and for all the prosperity that I procure unto it.
>
> —Jeremiah 33:9

> For how great is his goodness, and how great is his beauty! corn shall make the young men cheerful, and new wine the maids.
>
> —Zechariah 9:17

God's goodness is connected to fatness. Fatness is another picture of prosperity and abundance.

> Thou crownest the year with thy goodness; and thy paths drop fatness.
>
> —Psalm 65:11

The Excellence of Lebanon

The good land is a place of flourishing and growth. The good land includes Lebanon, a place of forests and trees. The trees of Lebanon represent excellence. We grow like the cedar in Lebanon in the good land. The good land is a place of excellence.

> Every place whereon the soles of your feet shall tread shall be yours: from the wilderness and Lebanon, from the river, the river Euphrates, even unto the uttermost sea shall your coast be.
>
> —Deuteronomy 11:24

> And all the drinking vessels of king Solomon were of gold, and all the vessels of the house of the forest of

> Lebanon were of pure gold: none were of silver; it was not any thing accounted of in the days of Solomon.
>
> —2 Chronicles 9:20

> The righteous shall flourish like the palm tree: he shall grow like a cedar in Lebanon.
>
> —Psalm 92:12

The trees of Lebanon are filled with sap, and sap is moisture.

> The trees of the Lord are full of sap; the cedars of Lebanon, which he hath planted.
>
> —Psalm 104:16

The trees of Lebanon are well watered. Lebanon is known for its cedars. The wood of Lebanon is good.

> King Solomon made himself a chariot of the wood of Lebanon.
>
> —Song of Solomon 3:9

Lebanon is mentioned in five scriptures in the Song of Solomon. Lebanon is a place of great beauty. The good land is full of the beauty of the Lord.

> Come with me from Lebanon, my spouse, with me from Lebanon: look from the top of Amana, from the top of Shenir and Hermon, from the lions' dens, from the mountains of the leopards.
>
> —Song of Solomon 4:8

> Thy lips, O my spouse, drop as the honeycomb: honey and milk are under thy tongue; and the smell of thy garments is like the smell of Lebanon.
>
> —Song of Solomon 4:11

Streams flow from the mountains of Lebanon. The good land is a land full of streams and rivers.

> A fountain of gardens, a well of living waters, and streams from Lebanon.
>
> —SONG OF SOLOMON 4:15

Lebanon represents excellence. The good land is a place of excellence.

> His legs are as pillars of marble, set upon sockets of fine gold: his countenance is as Lebanon, excellent as the cedars.
>
> —SONG OF SOLOMON 5:15

Lebanon was known for its towers. The Lord is our tower and stronghold.

> Thy neck is as a tower of ivory; thine eyes like the fishpools in Heshbon, by the gate of Bathrabbim: thy nose is as the tower of Lebanon which looketh toward Damascus.
>
> —SONG OF SOLOMON 7:4

Lebanon is a picture of glory. The good land is full of the glory of the Lord.

> It shall blossom abundantly, and rejoice even with joy and singing: the glory of Lebanon shall be given unto it, the excellency of Carmel and Sharon, they shall see the glory of the LORD, and the excellency of our God.
>
> —ISAIAH 35:2

The good land has snow. Snow is a picture of purity and cleansing. Lebanon is a place of snowcapped mountains.

> Will a man leave the snow of Lebanon which cometh from the rock of the field? or shall the cold flowing waters that come from another place be forsaken?
>
> —JEREMIAH 18:14

Snow is a picture of the word coming from heaven.

For as the heavens are higher than the earth, so are my ways higher than your ways, and my thoughts than your thoughts. For as the rain cometh down, and the snow from heaven, and returneth not thither, but watereth the earth, and maketh it bring forth and bud, that it may give seed to the sower, and bread to the eater: so shall my word be that goeth forth out of my mouth: it shall not return unto me void, but it shall accomplish that which I please, and it shall prosper in the thing whereto I sent it.

—Isaiah 55:9–11

Lebanon is a place of tall trees and deep roots.

I will be as the dew unto Israel: he shall grow as the lily, and cast forth his roots as Lebanon.

—Hosea 14:5

Lebanon represents beauty and a sweet smell.

His branches shall spread, and his beauty shall be as the olive tree, and his smell as Lebanon.

—Hosea 14:6

The good land has a good scent. There are no bad or unpleasant odors in the good land. Lebanon has good wine. The good land is a land of the wine of the Holy Spirit.

They that dwell under his shadow shall return; they shall revive as the corn, and grow as the vine: the scent thereof shall be as the wine of Lebanon.

—Hosea 14:7

Zion, the city of God, is in the good land. It is the New Jerusalem. It is the temple of God, the sanctuary, the church of the living God.

Thou shalt bring them in, and plant them in the mountain of thine inheritance, in the place, O Lord, which

thou hast made for thee to dwell in, in the Sanctuary,
O Lord, which thy hands have established. The Lord
shall reign for ever and ever.

—Exodus 15:17–18

Zion is the mountain of God. We come to this mountain in the good land. It is the place of God's rule and reign. It is the mountain of blessing and glory.

Isaiah tells us that Zion is also the place where God chooses to dwell. It is the place of His presence.

They shall not hurt nor destroy in all my holy mountain:
for the earth shall be full of the knowledge of the Lord,
as the waters cover the sea.

—Isaiah 11:9

The good land is the place of God's presence and glory. It is a land of peace and shalom.

Chapter 10

A LAND OF FEASTING AND JOY

PEACE OR SHALOM, joyful prayer, and feasting are what you can expect to experience as you move into the good land. Feasting and joy happen in the holy mountain of God. It is a feast of marrow and wine.

We have discussed how fat and fatness connect to the good land in terms of prosperity. In this case we are seeing it in connection with feasting and joy. In the good land we eat the fat and drink the sweet. Nehemiah told the Israelites to go and eat the fat (rich food).

> Then he said unto them, Go your way, eat the fat, and drink the sweet, and send portions unto them for whom nothing is prepared: for this day is holy unto our LORD: neither be ye sorry; for the joy of the LORD is your strength.
>
> —NEHEMIAH 8:10

Those who dwell in the good land have merry hearts. They are filled with joy and gladness. Maintaining a merry heart will give you a continual feast (eating the fat).

> All the days of the afflicted are evil: but he that is of a merry heart hath a continual feast.
>
> —PROVERBS 15:15

Jesus told the parable of the prodigal son. The son asked for his inheritance early and squandered it on riotous living. Upon his returning home, his father had the fatted calf killed. (See Luke 15:11–32.) The father's home was a type of the good land, and it was time for a celebration. The father was thrilled about his son's return and gave the best calf for he and his household to feast on.

> And bring hither the fatted calf, and kill it; and let us eat, and be merry.
>
> —Luke 15:23

The good land is a land of feasting. There is feasting and joy in the holy mountain. It is a feast of marrow and wine.

> And in this mountain shall the LORD of hosts make unto all people a feast of fat things, a feast of wines on the lees, of fat things full of marrow, of wines on the lees well refined.
>
> —Isaiah 25:6

> And on this Mount [Zion] shall the Lord of hosts make for all peoples a feast of rich things [symbolic of His coronation festival inaugurating the reign of the Lord on earth, in the wake of a background of gloom, judgment, and terror], a feast of wines on the lees—of fat things full of marrow, of wines on the lees well refined.
>
> —Isaiah 25:6, AMPC

A Place of Joy

The good land is not only a place of feasting but also a place of joy, peace, and righteousness in the Holy Ghost (Rom. 14:17). It is a place where we are strengthened by the joy of the Lord (Neh. 8:10). It is the place we come when we accept Christ. We come to the good land, to heavenly Zion, the heavenly city. We are born of that city. We are born from above.

The good land is a place of worship and glory and the mountain of God. It is a place of God's presence. It is a high place. It is a place of celebration and life in the Spirit, where our expectations are exceeded and we find joy and satisfaction, favor, blessing, acceptance, and love.

It's Spirit-filled living. It is a place where we are free to enjoy God and His presence. It's enjoying life in His city, His land—the place from which all our enemies have been driven out.

It is a place of joyful prayer.

> Even them will I bring to my holy mountain, and make them joyful in my house of prayer: their burnt offerings and their sacrifices shall be accepted upon mine altar; for mine house shall be called an house of prayer for all people.
>
> —ISAIAH 56:7

Prayer is full of joy in the good land because we know that as we pray in faith, we have what we ask of God. We do not ask amiss. Our prayers are on target with the heart of the King.

Chapter 11

A LAND OF REST

FINALLY, THE GOOD land is a land of rest. We enjoy rest from our enemies in the good land. We dwell in safety in the good land. The people of Israel did not enter into God's rest due to their unbelief, but we can enter into it by faith in Christ—the same faith we need to enter into the good land, where true rest can be enjoyed.

As we have discovered in part 1 of this book, the good land is for those who are willing and obedient. Isaiah 1:19 says, "If ye be willing and obedient, ye shall eat the good of the land." As we obey God and follow Him to the land He shows us, He will lead us into a place of rest. This rest comes once we have gone through the wilderness, which is a type of deliverance, and by clearing the land of all spiritual enemies upon arrival. We can then enjoy rest and dwell in safety.

> But when ye go over Jordan, and dwell in the land which the LORD your God giveth you to inherit, and when he giveth you rest from all your enemies round about, so that ye dwell in safety.
>
> —DEUTERONOMY 12:10
>
> And in this place again, if they shall enter into my rest.
>
> —HEBREWS 4:5

> For he that is entered into his rest, he also hath ceased
> from his own works, as God did from his. Let us labour
> therefore to enter into that rest, lest any man fall after
> the same example of unbelief.
>
> —HEBREWS 4:10–11

We rest in the Lord's finished work. We rest in His love.
There is no striving, no anxiety, and no fear in the good land.

> Come unto me, all ye that labour and are heavy laden,
> and I will give you rest.
>
> —MATTHEW 11:28

We are able to rest in the good land because we obey God
and keep His commands. He will allow us to eat the good or
best when we are willing and obedient. The Amplified version
of Isaiah 1:19 says, "If you are willing and obedient, you shall
eat the best of the land." The Living Bible says, "If you will
only let me help you, if you will only obey, then I will make
you rich!"

Willingness and obedience are the keys to enjoying the best.
Are you willing to do the will of God? Are you obedient to the
Word of God and His plans for your life? If your answer is yes,
then you are in position to receive God's best.

God gave His people the best land. Numbers 14:7 tells us that
"they spake unto all the company of the children of Israel, saying,
The land, which we passed through to search it, is an exceeding
good land." The Voice translation of the same verse says that the
land God gave Israel was "some of the best land ever."

The Choicest Blessings

God chooses our inheritance for us. He gives us the best. He
gives us His choicest blessings. Psalm 47:4 says, "He shall
choose our inheritance for us, the excellency of Jacob whom he
loved. Selah." The Living Bible says God "will personally select

his choicest blessings for his Jewish people—the very best for those he loves."

> Your pleasant path leads me to pleasant places. I'm overwhelmed by the privileges that come with following you, for you have given me the best!
>
> —Psalm 16:6, tpt

> Keep showing the humble your path, and lead them into the best decision. Bring revelation-light that trains them in the truth.
>
> —Psalm 25:9, tpt

There are many paths a person can choose. It is important to choose and walk in the best path, which God will show you as you seek Him.

> I will instruct you (says the Lord) and guide you along the best pathway for your life; I will advise you and watch your progress.
>
> —Psalm 32:8, tlb

God's paths drop fatness. Fatness is plenty, prosperity, abundance, and riches. Fatness is a picture of the best.

> Thou crownest the year with thy goodness; and thy paths drop fatness.
>
> —Psalm 65:11

God's paths lead to the best. You can walk on a good path. Wisdom leads you in the best path for your life.

> Then shalt thou understand righteousness, and judgment, and equity; yea, every good path.
>
> —Proverbs 2:9

Leanness and Judgment

Fatness is compared to leanness in Scripture. *Leanness* means "spare, lank, lanky, gaunt, rawboned, scrawny, skinny...thin because of an absence of excess flesh. *Lean* stresses lack of fat and of curving contours."[1]

> And the lean and the ill favored cows ate up the seven fat cows that had come first.
>
> —GENESIS 41:20, AMPC

Pharaoh had a dream of lean cattle eating up fat cattle. Joseph interpreted the dream to represent seven years of famine that would follow seven years of prosperity. Leanness or thinness is a picture of famine and lack. Fatness is a picture of abundance and prosperity. Leanness can be the result of pining. *Pining* means "languishing; drooping; wasting away, as with longing; wasting; consuming."[2]

God gave the people meat in the wilderness but sent leanness to their souls. Leanness is the opposite of fatness.

> And he gave them their request; but sent leanness into their soul.
>
> —PSALM 106:15

Leanness is a picture of judgment.

> Therefore shall the Lord, the Lord of hosts, send among his fat ones leanness; and under his glory he shall kindle a burning like the burning of a fire.
>
> —ISAIAH 10:16

> And in that day it shall come to pass, that the glory of Jacob shall be made thin, and the fatness of his flesh shall wax lean.
>
> —ISAIAH 17:4

> Therefore thus saith the Lord GOD unto them; Behold,
> I, even I, will judge between the fat cattle and between
> the lean cattle.
>
> —EZEKIEL 34:20

Man's bones stick out (leanness) because of God's chastening.

> He is chastened also with pain upon his bed, and the
> multitude of his bones with strong pain...his flesh is
> consumed away, that it cannot be seen; and his bones
> that were not seen stick out.
>
> —JOB 33:19, 21

David humbled himself and repented through fasting. His
flesh failed of fatness. This is a picture of sadness and sorrow.

> My knees are weak through fasting; and my flesh faileth
> of fatness.
>
> —PSALM 109:24

Leanness comes through famine. Again, this is a picture of
judgment. Throughout the Book of Jeremiah the prophet wept
over the condition of Israel and its coming judgment.

> Their visage is blacker than a coal; they are not known in
> the streets: their skin cleaveth to their bones; it is with-
> ered, it is become like a stick.
>
> —LAMENTATIONS 4:8

Fatness is associated with a table. Our table is blessed when
it has fatness.

> Even so would he have removed thee out of the strait
> into a broad place, where there is no straitness; and that
> which should be set on thy table should be full of fatness.
>
> —JOB 36:16

God prepares a table for us in the presence of our enemies
(Ps. 23:5). Wisdom provides a table (Prov. 9:1–2). The root

word of *table* (*shulchan*) in Hebrew is *shalach*, which means to "shoot forth, grow long, reach forth, sow, spread, stretch."[3] It is a common Hebrew word that also means to send forth.[4]

In the New Testament the word translated "send" and "send forth" is *apostello*, which is where we get our English word *apostle*.[5] An apostle is one who is sent forth for a purpose. In the first-century church and even until this day, apostles are those who establish churches and the order in which the presbytery of the church functions.

Apostolic ministries should provide rich food that will help you grow "fat." The apostolic anointing will help you burst your bonds and destroy yokes.

Another Hebrew word for *fatten* is *abas*, which means "to feed."[6] God has promised to feed us.

> Trust in the LORD, and do good; so shalt thou dwell in the land, and verily thou shalt be fed.
>
> —PSALM 37:3

God feeds us with the finest (fat) of the wheat (Ps. 81:16). The elders are charged with the assignment to "feed the flock of God" (1 Pet. 5:2).

> Save thy people, and bless thine inheritance: feed them also, and lift them up for ever.
>
> —PSALM 28:9

God prepares a table for us and feeds us from His table. God makes us fat, flourishing, and healthy. The yokes are destroyed because of the fat.

Butter and Honey

I introduced the concept of honey and butter as representatives of prosperity in chapter 6. Here butter shows up again in relationship to fatness. Job described his prosperity in terms of butter.

> When I washed my steps with butter, and the rock poured me out rivers of oil.
>
> —Job 29:6

The Expanded Bible says, "It was as if my path [or steps] were covered with cream [or butter] and the rocks poured out olive oil for me [representing his earlier prosperity]."

Eating butter and honey is another symbol of fatness and prosperity.

> And it shall come to pass, for the abundance of milk that they shall give he shall eat butter: for butter and honey shall every one eat that is left in the land.
>
> —Isaiah 7:22

Butter comes from an abundance of milk. Butter is the cream or curd of the milk. Butter is known for its richness and fatness. Notice that butter is mentioned as one of the blessings of the land of promise. Butter is mentioned with fat and the blood of grapes.

> Butter of kine [cows], and milk of sheep, with fat of lambs, and rams of the breed of Bashan, and goats, with the fat of kidneys of wheat; and thou didst drink the pure blood of the grape.
>
> —Deuteronomy 32:14

The Message translation of Psalm 81:16 says, "You'll feast on my fresh-baked bread spread with butter and rock-pure honey."

God increased His people greatly and made them stronger than their enemies. Your enemy will not be able to hold you in bondage.

And he increased his people greatly; and made them stronger than their enemies.

—PSALM 105:24

Bones, Marrow, and Fatness

Fatness is connected to marrow (Ps. 63:5). Marrow is connected to the bones. God can make our bones fat (Isa. 58:11). Healthy bones have healthy marrow, which in turn produces healthy blood. Healthy blood is a key to a healthy body and good health. Wisdom is health to our navel and marrow to our bones (Prov. 3:8). Good news puts fat on the bones (Prov. 15:30). We can also lose ourselves from the bands of our neck. Remember the anointing (fat) destroys the yoke. The anointing gives you a large neck.

> Shake thyself from the dust; arise, and sit down, O Jerusalem: loose thyself from the bands of thy neck, O captive daughter of Zion.
>
> —ISAIAH 52:2

Zion is called to be strong and free. You are Zion. *Fatness* is another word for prosperity. You can break free through prosperity.

> The liberal soul shall be made fat: and he that watereth shall be watered also himself.
>
> —PROVERBS 11:25

The New International Version translates this verse, "a generous person will prosper." I believe that giving will make you "fat" financially. Giving is a way to break off the yoke of poverty and lack. The Hebrew word *dashen* means "to be fat, grow fat…become greasy, become prosperous."[7] *Dashen* is the word used in Psalm 23:5 and is translated "anointest." Here is the expanded definition of *dashen*: "a primitive root;

to be fat; transitively, to fatten (or regard as fat); specifically to anoint; figuratively, to satisfy; denominatively (from *deshen*) to remove (fat) ashes (of sacrifices)—accept, anoint, take away the (receive) ashes (from), make (wax) fat."[8]

Are You Enjoying the Good Land?

You have now been introduced to the revelation of the good land. You've been taken through the scriptures that show the characteristics of life in the land God has chosen for you. The question is, Are you enjoying the good land? If you have received salvation through faith in Jesus Christ, you should be enjoying life in the Spirit of God. If you're not and you are feeling stuck in the wilderness of life, it may be time for you to leave where you are and, like Abraham, venture out to a place God will show you. Perhaps it is a group of friends, a job, or a church that is no longer serving the new season you are embarking on. I pray that this book is opening your eyes to things God may be trying to speak to your heart about what is next for you.

If you are not saved, or if you have backslidden, the invitation to accept or return to Christ and enter the good land is always open to you. In Matthew 11:28–29 Jesus says, "Come unto me, all ye that labour and are heavy laden, and I will give you rest. Take my yoke upon you, and learn of me; for I am meek and lowly in heart: and ye shall find rest unto your souls." Rest from your enemies, rest from the worries and cares of life, and rest from barely making it one day to the next can be yours in the good land. Unlike the yoke of the world, Christ's yoke is easy. He increases you so much until no yokes of bondage can hold you back. Words that others have spoken over you—dream stealers, naysayers, and people who just don't see the greatness in you—will be broken off your life as you come into the good land.

Whatever spiritual position you find yourself in, if you are not enjoying the good land, God is calling you out. Abraham was told to leave his country, the place where he grew up, and go to a place that God would show him. God revealed to Abraham there was something bigger than he had lived before. God is saying, "There is a city I have built, a city with a foundation. It is Zion. I Am the builder. I Am the maker. I'm going to show you something beyond the natural land or possessions you desire. It is something heavenly and supernatural."

I encourage you to pray and speak out the confessions in the conclusion coming up next so you can begin to build a faith like Abraham's to live in this land of promise just as he did. And just as Abraham was looking beyond the physical place to which God had led him, God wants you to see that He has something greater for you. He wants you to see the greater—that something greater is the fulfillment of the good land through Jesus Christ.

Conclusion

CONFESS IT—THE GOOD LAND IS YOUR LAND

GOD WANTS YOU to have the best. He has set aside a place for you called the good land. As you have learned about this place and what it takes to dwell there, I encourage you to begin to appropriate it by faith. Confess the promises that have been laid out for you and expect nothing but the best. Be ready to follow God to the new land. Don't allow Lots to slow you down. Pursue the good land, the place of peace, prosperity, enlargement, bounty, beauty, and rest from all your enemies.

As I studied this topic, God led me to various confessions, prayers, and declarations that activate faith and expectancy. I have placed them here in the concluding portion of this book. These good land confessions lead you to humbly submit to God's will for your life and the path of goodness He intends for you.

Good Land Confessions

I am willing and obedient, and I will eat the good of the land. I enter the good land by faith.

The good land is my inheritance in Christ.

I enjoy the blessing and prosperity of the good land. The river of God flows into my life.

The rain of heaven falls upon my life. My harvest is plentiful.

I lack nothing in the good land. I drink the milk and eat the honey. I am nourished in the good land. I enjoy the sweetness of the Lord. I come to the mountain of God.

I am a part of Zion.

I live under the rule and reign of God. I enjoy God's goodness in this land.

I am like a cedar of Lebanon.

The hills drop new wine in my life. I enjoy the fatness of the Lord.

I drink from the fountain of living waters. I enjoy the finest of the wheat.

I enjoy the fruits of the land. There is a good scent in my life. I wash my steps in butter.

The rock pours out rivers of oil for me. I am anointed with fresh oil.

I eat and I am satisfied.

I praise God for His goodness in this land.

The glory of the Lord is upon my life in the good land. I live in a wealthy place.

I live in a large place.

The heavens are open over my life.

The Lord opens unto me His good treasure. I receive an abundance of rain.

I enjoy the new wine of the Spirit. I sit under my own fig tree.

I have my own vineyard. I will lend and not borrow.

I enjoy a continual feast in the good land.

The beauty of the Lord is upon my life. I have beauty for ashes.

I walk in the strength and comfort of the Lord. I enter into rest in the good land.

I live in safety in the good land. The dew of heaven is upon my life.

The word from heaven drops upon my life. My life is filled with moisture and sap.

I am a tree of righteousness, the planting of the Lord. I enjoy good things.

There is no famine in my life.

I am Abraham's seed and heir according to the promise. Through meekness I inherit the land.

Confessions for the Best

The best is yet to come.

I will walk into the best.

I release my faith for the best.

My worst days and years are behind me.

I serve the God of the best.

May the Lord command the best for my life.

My God is the best, and He gives me the best.

I live in the land, and I enjoy the best.

I am favored with the best.

My God knows what is best for me.

I will live my best life.

I will live and walk in excellence.

I will pursue and desire what is excellent.

I will approve things that are excellent.

I will have an excellent spirit.

Let excellent glory be on my life.

My God will do excellent things in my life.

Let heaven release the best blessings over my life.

Let my life overflow with the best.

God's ways are the best ways for my life.

God's plans are the best plans for my future.

I will be willing and obedient, and I will eat the best of the land.

God chooses my inheritance and gives me the best.

This will be one of the best years of my life.

I will make the best choices.

My God teaches me to profit and leads me in the way I should go.

My finances will be the best.

I will enjoy God's best.

I will eat the finest of the wheat.

I will make the best decisions.

I will walk in the best paths

I will enjoy fatness and marrow in the house of the Lord.

I will receive the best blessings.

I will give the Lord my best.

I will give Him my best praise and worship.

I will receive the best ministry.

I will give the best offerings.

My thinking will be the best.

My speaking will be the best.

I will understand things that are excellent.

I will speak things that are excellent.

I will have the best:

- The best relationships
- The best sleep and rest
- The best peace (shalom)
- The best fellowship
- The best ideas
- The best wisdom
- The best understanding
- The best gifts
- The best breakthroughs
- The best doors
- The best health
- The best vision
- The best hope
- The best desires
- The best motives
- The best plans
- The best insight
- The best discernment
- The best discounts
- The best surprises
- The best increase
- The best promotions
- The best oil (anointing)
- The best wine (move of the Spirit)
- The best help
- The best assignments
- The best alignments

- The best organization
- The best order
- The best timing
- The best gatherings
- The best communication
- The best teaching
- The best preaching
- The best thoughts
- The best music
- The best songs
- The best marriages
- The best inventions
- The best progress

- The best changes
- The best moves
- The best successes
- The best counsel
- The best course of action
- The best harvest
- The best impact
- The best protection
- The best safety
- The best creativity
- The best innovation
- The best investments

Fat and Flourishing Confessions

I am like a green olive tree in the house of the Lord.

I will be satisfied with marrow and fatness.

I will enjoy the fatness of God's house.

I will be fat and flourishing.

The anointing in my life destroys all yokes.

I am growing large and increasing, and I burst every yoke.

My neck is too large for the yokes of the enemy.

I enjoy the fatness of the kingdom.

I feast on what is fat and good.

God prepares a table before me.

I eat at God's table.

God feeds me and makes me strong.

I am liberal, and I am made fat.

My bones are fat and flourishing.

I break every yoke because of prosperity.

I enjoy abundance and prosperity.

I receive and walk in God's best for my life.

I eat the fat and drink the sweet, and the joy of the Lord is my strength.

God anoints my head with oil, and my cup runs over.

I dwell in the land, and I am fed.

I enjoy the fat of the land.

Appendix

ADDITIONAL SCRIPTURES ON THE GOOD LAND

Save when there shall be no poor among you; for the LORD shall greatly bless thee in the land which the LORD thy God giveth thee for an inheritance to possess it.

—DEUTERONOMY 15:4

Moses my servant is dead; now therefore arise, go over this Jordan, thou, and all this people, unto the land which I do give to them, even to the children of Israel. Every place that the sole of your foot shall tread upon, that have I given unto you, as I said unto Moses.

—JOSHUA 1:2–3

Trust in the LORD, and do good; so shalt thou dwell in the land, and verily thou shalt be fed.

—PSALM 37:3

For evildoers shall be cut off: but those that wait upon the LORD, they shall inherit the earth.

—PSALM 37:9

But the meek shall inherit the earth; and shall delight themselves in the abundance of peace.

—PSALM 37:11

For such as be blessed of him shall inherit the earth; and they that be cursed of him shall be cut off.

—PSALM 37:22

The righteous shall inherit the land, and dwell therein for ever.

—PSALM 37:29

Wait on the LORD, and keep his way, and he shall exalt thee to inherit the land: when the wicked are cut off, thou shalt see it.

—PSALM 37:34

For they got not the land in possession by their own sword, neither did their own arm save them: but thy right hand, and thine arm, and the light of thy countenance, because thou hadst a favour unto them.

—PSALM 44:3

Surely his salvation is nigh them that fear him; that glory may dwell in our land.

—PSALM 85:9

Yea, the LORD shall give that which is good; and our land shall yield her increase.

—PSALM 85:12

The righteous shall never be removed: but the wicked shall not inhabit the earth.

—PROVERBS 10:30

The flowers appear on the earth; the time of the singing of birds is come, and the voice of the turtle is heard in our land.

—SONG OF SOLOMON 2:12

In that day shall this song be sung in the land of Judah; we have a strong city; salvation will God appoint for walls and bulwarks.

—Isaiah 26:1

Thy people also shall be all righteous: they shall inherit the land for ever, the branch of my planting, the work of my hands, that I may be glorified.

—Isaiah 60:21

For your shame ye shall have double; and for confusion they shall rejoice in their portion: therefore in their land they shall possess the double: everlasting joy shall be unto them.

—Isaiah 61:7

Thou shalt no more be termed Forsaken; neither shall thy land any more be termed Desolate: but thou shalt be called Hephzibah, and thy land Beulah: for the Lord delighteth in thee, and thy land shall be married.

—Isaiah 62:4

And I will make with them a covenant of peace, and will cause the evil beasts to cease out of the land: and they shall dwell safely in the wilderness, and sleep in the woods....And the tree of the field shall yield her fruit, and the earth shall yield her increase, and they shall be safe in their land, and shall know that I am the Lord, when I have broken the bands of their yoke, and delivered them out of the hand of those that served themselves of them. And they shall no more be a prey to the heathen, neither shall the beast of the land devour them; but they shall dwell safely, and none shall make them afraid.

—Ezekiel 34:25–28

And ye shall dwell in the land that I gave to your fathers; and ye shall be my people, and I will be your God.

—Ezekiel 36:28

Therefore prophesy and say unto them, Thus saith the Lord GOD; Behold, O my people, I will open your graves, and cause you to come up out of your graves, and bring you into the land of Israel....And shall put my spirit in you, and ye shall live, and I shall place you in your own land: then shall ye know that I the LORD have spoken it, and performed it, saith the LORD.

—EZEKIEL 37:12–14

Fear not, O land; be glad and rejoice: for the LORD will do great things.

—JOEL 2:21

And all nations shall call you blessed: for ye shall be a delightsome land, saith the LORD of hosts.

—MALACHI 3:12

Blessed are the meek: for they shall inherit the earth.

—MATTHEW 5:5

Great blessings belong to those who are humble. They will be given the land God promised.

—MATTHEW 5:5, ERV

NOTES

Introduction
The Good Land Revelation

1. Blue Letter Bible, s.v. *"gē,"* accessed July 29, 2019, https://www.blueletterbible.org/lang/lexicon/lexicon. cfm?Strongs=G1093&t=KJV.

Chapter 1
Possessing the Land

1. Blue Letter Bible, s.v. *"ʽanag,"* accessed July 29, 2019, https://www.blueletterbible.org/lang/lexicon/lexicon. cfm?Strongs=H6026&t=KJV.

2. Blue Letter Bible, s.v. *"ʽanav,"* accessed July 29, 2019, https://www.blueletterbible.org/lang/lexicon/lexicon. cfm?Strongs=H6035&t=KJV.

Chapter 2
Coming Into God's Best

1. Andrew Wommack, "Living in God's Best—Don't Settle for Less," Andrew Wommack Ministries, accessed July 29, 2019, https://www.awmi.net/reading/teaching-articles/ receive_best/.

2. Christine A. Lindberg, ed., *Oxford American Writer's Thesaurus, 3rd ed.* (New York: Oxford University Press, 2012), s.v. "best," accessed July 29, 2019, https://books. google.com/books?id=f_xMAgAAQBAJ&q=80#v=snippet& q=best&f=false.

3. Blue Letter Bible, s.v. *"cheleb,"* accessed July 29, 2019, https://www.blueletterbible.org/lang/lexicon/lexicon. cfm?Strongs=H2459&t=KJV.

4. Sam Oluwatoki, "The Finest of Wheat," *The Word* (blog), August 1, 2016, https://brosamueloluwatoki.wordpress.com/2016/08/01/the-finest-of-wheat/.

5. Bible Hub, s.v. "Psalm 81:16," accessed July 29, 2019, https://biblehub.com/commentaries/barnes/psalms/81.htm.

6. Rich Doebler, "Opening Our Heart to Believe for God's Best" (sermon, Journey Christian Church, Cloquet, MN, January 19, 2014), http://www.cloquetchurch.com/2014/01/opening-our-heart-to-believe-for-gods-best/.

7. *Lexico*, s.v. "virtue," accessed July 29, 2019, https://www.lexico.com/en/synonym/virtue.

8. Joseph Prince, *100 Days of Favor* (Lake Mary, FL: Charisma House, 2011), 269.

Chapter 5
A Large and Wealthy Place

1. "Why Is the Fat Reserved for God?," The Simple Answers, accessed July 29, 2019, https://www.thesimpleanswers.com/articles/2007/12/09/why-is-the-fat-reserved-for-god/.

2. "Why Is the Fat Reserved for God?," The Simple Answers.

3. Blue Letter Bible, s.v. *"cheleb."*

4. Chaim and Laura Bentorah, "Word Study—Fat and Kicking," Chaim Bentorah, August 18, 2015, https://www.chaimbentorah.com/2015/08/word-study-fat-and-kicking-%D7%99%EF%AC%AA%D7%A1%D7%9F-%D7%95%D7%99%D7%91%D7%A2%D7%98/?print=print.

Chapter 6
A Land of Milk and Honey

1. Jonathan Cohen, "Why Milk and Honey," accessed July 29, 2019, https://www.uhmc.sunysb.edu/surgery/m&h.html.

2. Jane Birch, "A Land Flowing With 'Milk and Honey,'" Discovering the Word of Wisdom, February 18, 2019,

https://discoveringthewordofwisdom.com/about/the-word-of-wisdom/wow-faqs/milk-and-honey/.

Chapter 8
A Land Where the Anointing Flows Like Oil

1.   Michael Brown, "A Hebrew Insight That Breaks the Yoke," Charisma News, May 31, 2013, https://www.charismanews.com/opinion/39700-a-hebrew-insight-that-breaks-the-yoke.
2.   Brad Sullivan, "Anointing," Brad Sullivan Ministries, February 22, 2018, http://bradsullivan.org/anointing/.
3.   Sullivan, "Anointing."
4.   Harold Miller Jr., "The Anointing That Destroys the Yoke?," A Word in Season, June 4, 2013, https://haroldmillerjr.com/2013/06/04/the-anointing-that-destroys-the-yoke/.
5.   Michelle Corral, "The Institute of the Anointing: The Supernatural Secret of the Anointing in Your Life," accessed July 29, 2019, https://myemail.constantcontact.com/The-Supernatural-Secret-of-the-Anointing-in-Your-Life.html?soid=1108609739633&aid=x0GVuxsMuYQ.
6.   *Lexico*, s.v. "burst," accessed July 29, 2019, https://www.lexico.com/en/definition/burst.

Chapter 11
A Land of Rest

1.   Merriam-Webster, s.v. "lean," accessed July 29, 2019, https://www.merriam-webster.com/dictionary/leanness.
2.   Bible Hub, s.v. "pining," accessed July 29, 2019, https://biblehub.com/topical/p/pining.htm.
3.   Blue Letter Bible, s.v. "*shalach*," accessed July 29, 2019, https://www.blueletterbible.org/lang/lexicon/lexicon.cfm?strongs=H7971&t=KJV.
4.   Brad Scott, "Table," Wildbranch Ministry, accessed July 29, 2019, https://www.wildbranch.org/teachings/word-studies/19table.html.

5. Blue Letter Bible, s.v. "apostellō," accessed July 31, 2019, https://www.blueletterbible.org/lang/Lexicon/lexicon.cfm?strongs=G649&t=KJV.

6. Bible Hub, s.v. *"abas,"* accessed July 29, 2019, https://biblehub.com/hebrew/75.htm. https://www.blueletterbible.org/kjv/eph/4/11/s_1101011

7. Bible Hub, s.v. *"dashen,"* accessed July 29, 2019, https://biblehub.com/hebrew/1878.htm.

8. Bible Hub, s.v. *"dashen."*